M000268168

IT MATTERS
52 DEVOTIONS TO
STRENGTHEN KIDMIN LEADERS

BETH FRANK

KIDZMATTER
PUBLISHING

It Matters: 52 Devotions to Strengthen Kidmin Leaders

© 2023 by Beth Frank. All rights reserved.

Published by KidzMatter
432 East Val Lane, Marion, IN 46952

Printed in the United States of America

All rights reserved. No part of this publication may be reproduced, stored in a retrieval system, or transmitted in any form or by any means-for example, electronic, photocopy, recording-without the prior written permission of the publisher. The only exception is brief quotations in printed reviews.

Scriptures taken from the Holy Bible, New International Version®, NIV®. Copyright © 1973, 1978, 1984, 2011 by Biblica, Inc.™ Used by permission of Zondervan. All rights reserved worldwide. www.zondervan.com The "NIV" and "New International Version" are trademarks registered in the United States Patent and Trademark Office by Biblica, Inc.™

Original Conference Theme by twelve:thirty Media -https://twelvethirty.media
Cover adapted by Nicole Jones - kneecoalgrace@gmail.com
Interior layout by Nicole Jones - kneecoalgrace@gmail.com

ISBN: 978-1-0882-4920-8

INTRODUCTION

Dear Kidmin Friend,

Welcome to "It Matters: A Kidmin Devotional!" This book is specifically crafted for you—the incredible children's ministry leaders, teachers, and volunteers—who pour your hearts into serving children and families. I believe that what you do in kids' ministry matters immensely, and this devotional aims to explore why.

In the following pages, we will delve into six key reasons why kids' ministry holds such incredible significance. Each point reinforces the value and impact of your dedication to guiding children in their spiritual growth and nurturing their relationship with God.

It Matters to God: Above all else, kids' ministry matters to God. Jesus Himself expressed the importance of children when He said, "Let the little children come to me, and do not hinder them, for the kingdom of heaven belongs to such as these." (Matthew 19:14). By investing in the spiritual formation of children, you are directly participating in God's work of shaping young hearts.

It Matters to the Church: Kids' ministry is an essential part of the larger body of Christ. The Bible teaches that believers are one body with many parts, and children are a vital component. By nurturing their faith, you contribute to the growth and vitality of the entire church community.

It Matters to Families: Kids' ministry provides invaluable support to families. As you come alongside parents and guardians, you offer a helping hand in raising their children in the ways of the Lord. By equipping families with tools, resources, and a supportive community, you strengthen the family unit and encourage a flourishing faith at home.

It Matters to Kids: Kids' ministry matters to the children themselves. In their formative years, they are building a foundation of faith that will shape their entire lives. By providing a safe, nurturing environment where they can encounter God's love, you have the privilege of igniting a lifelong journey of faith.

It Matters to Your Community and the World: Kids' ministry extends its impact beyond the church walls. As children grow in their faith, they become ambassadors of God's love and light in their communities. By instilling biblical values and a heart for service, you empower children to make a positive difference in the world.

It Matters to the Future: Children are not only the future of the church but also eternal beings. By investing in their spiritual growth today, you are shaping their destinies for eternity. Kids' ministry has the power to leave a lasting legacy that extends far beyond this earthly life.

In each devotion, we will explore these six points further, providing encouragement, inspiration, and practical insights to fuel your ministry. Remember, what you do in kids' ministry truly matters—to God, the church, families, kids themselves, your community, the world, and eternity. So, let's dive in and discover the incredible significance of your role in nurturing the next generation of believers. It definitely matters!

XO,
Beth

CHILDREN'S MINISTRY
IS NOT JUST A
PROGRAM; IT'S A

calling

TO SHAPE HEARTS
AND CHANGE LIVES.

WEEK 1: IT MATTERS TO GOD
God's Heart for Kids Ministry

"But Jesus said, 'Let the little children come to me, and do not hinder them, for the kingdom of heaven belongs to such as these.'"
Matthew 19:14

God's love for children is profound and unwavering. Throughout the Bible, we see evidence of His tender care for the young ones among us. Jesus Himself demonstrated this love when He welcomed the children and declared that the kingdom of heaven belongs to them. In this devotional series, we will explore the big picture of why kids' ministry is important to God. Let's dive in and discover the heart of our Heavenly Father.

As we begin our journey into understanding God's heart for kids' ministry, let's reflect on the significance of children in His kingdom. Children possess a remarkable capacity for faith, trust, and wonder. Their hearts are open, receptive, and willing to believe in the unseen. Jesus recognized this and celebrated their innocence and humility as essential qualities for entering the kingdom of heaven.

When we engage in kids' ministry, we are privileged to nurture and cultivate these qualities. We have the opportunity to sow seeds of faith, love, and truth into their lives. By teaching them about God's Word and His love for them, we help lay a solid foundation for their spiritual growth.

Just as a master artist envisions a breathtaking masterpiece, God sees the potential within each child. He longs to transform their lives, shaping them into vessels of His glory. When we invest our time, energy, and resources into kids' ministry, we participate in the divine work of shaping young hearts for eternity.

Take a moment to reflect on the children in your life or the ones you minister to. Consider the unique qualities they possess and the incredible potential they hold. Today, let's thank God for entrusting us with the responsibility of guiding them closer to Him.

Dear Heavenly Father, thank You for the gift of children. We recognize their significance in Your kingdom and the potential they hold. Help us to be faithful stewards of the little ones You have entrusted to us. Give us wisdom, patience, and love as we guide them in their journey of faith. May our efforts in kids' ministry reflect Your heart and bring glory to Your name. In Jesus' name, we pray. Amen.

Takeaway

Children are not just the future of the church but also important members of God's kingdom today. As we embark on this series of devotionals, let's approach kids' ministry with a renewed sense of purpose and appreciation for the role we play in shaping their spiritual journeys. IT MATTERS.

_____

_____

_____

_____

_____

_____

_____

_____

IN CHILDREN'S MINISTRY,
WE HAVE THE PRIVILEGE OF

sowing seeds

OF FAITH THAT WILL BEAR FRUIT
FOR ETERNITY.

WEEK 2 : IT MATTERS TO GOD
Being Faithful in Your Calling

"Moreover, it is required of stewards that they be found faithful."
1 Corinthians 4:2

In 1 Corinthians 4:2, the apostle Paul speaks of the requirement for stewards to be found faithful. As children's ministry leaders, teachers, and volunteers, we are stewards of God's precious little ones. We have been entrusted with the responsibility of nurturing their faith, guiding them in their spiritual journey, and pointing them to Jesus. Our faithfulness in this calling is not to be taken lightly.

Faithfulness in ministry involves several key aspects. Firstly, it requires commitment. We are called to be steadfast and dedicated in our service to God and His children. This means showing up consistently, being present in the lives of the children we serve, and faithfully teaching them God's Word.

Secondly, faithfulness in ministry requires perseverance. Kids' Ministry can be challenging at times. It may involve dealing with difficult behaviors, facing obstacles, or encountering moments of doubt. However, when we persevere in the face of adversity, relying on God's strength and wisdom, we demonstrate our faithfulness to Him.

Thirdly, faithfulness in ministry entails wholehearted devotion. It is not just about fulfilling a duty; it is about pouring our hearts and souls into the lives of the children entrusted to us. It means praying for them, listening to them, and being sensitive to their unique needs. It means going above and beyond to create an environment where they can encounter God's love and grow in their faith.

Our faithfulness in Kids' Ministry is deeply important to God because it reflects His heart for ministry and His love for children. God's Word is filled with examples of His concern for the younger generation.

When we are faithful in our calling, we become vessels through which God's love and truth flow into the lives of children. Our faithfulness plants seeds of faith, love, and hope that can take root and grow, impacting children's lives for years to come. Through our faithfulness, we become instruments in shaping young hearts, allowing them to experience God's transformative power.

As you reflect on your role in Kids' Ministry, consider the ways in which you can be more faithful in your calling. Seek God's guidance and strength to remain committed, persevere through challenges, and devote yourself wholeheartedly to the children you serve. Your faithfulness is not in vain; it matters to God, and it matters to the children whose lives you touch.

Dear Heavenly Father, thank You for the privilege of serving in Kids Ministry. Help us to be faithful stewards of the little ones You have entrusted to us. Strengthen us in our commitment, grant us perseverance, and ignite within us a wholehearted devotion to the children we serve. May our faithfulness reflect Your heart for ministry and bring glory to Your name. In Jesus' name, we pray. Amen.

Takeaway

Being faithful in your calling to Kids' Ministry is an expression of your love for God and His children. Remember that your faithfulness matters as you strive to be steadfast, persevere, and wholeheartedly devote yourself to the children you serve. It aligns with God's heart for ministry and His deep love for children. May your faithfulness be a shining testimony of God's grace and transform lives for His glory. IT MATTERS.

_____

_____

_____

_____

_____

_____

_____

_____

CHILDREN'S MINISTRY
IS WHERE LITTLE HANDS MEET
THE HANDS OF

Jesus.

WEEK 3 : IT MATTERS TO GOD
Unlocking Hearts in a Safe Harbor

"Whoever welcomes one of these little children in my name welcomes me, and whoever welcomes me does not welcome me but the one who sent me."
Mark 9:37

In Mark 9:37, Jesus speaks about the profound connection between welcoming a child and welcoming Him. He teaches us that when we embrace children in His name, we are not only showing love and acceptance to them but also demonstrating our love and acceptance of Jesus Himself. It is a powerful reminder of the significance of how we welcome children into our ministry.

Creating a loving environment involves more than just a warm greeting; it requires an atmosphere of genuine care, respect, and acceptance. When children step into our ministry spaces, they should feel a sense of belonging and safety. They should encounter love that reflects the unconditional love of their Heavenly Father.

We are privileged to be the hands and feet of Jesus as we welcome children into our ministry. We have the opportunity to model His love, grace, and kindness. By listening attentively, offering encouraging words, and being present in their lives, we create a space where they can grow, thrive, and experience the love of Christ.

Furthermore, creating a safe learning environment is crucial. Children need to feel physically and emotionally secure in order to engage fully in their spiritual growth. We must prioritize their well-being and take measures to protect them from harm. By establishing clear boundaries, implementing safety protocols, and nurturing an environment of trust, we enable children to explore their faith with confidence.

As a mom of a special needs daughter, I would love to interject here that this principle applies to all types and ability levels. Each and every child should have the opportunity and blessing of knowing they have a place where they are safe, loved, and belong. It blesses my heart to think of the church providing that space and place for specially-abled kiddos.

15

In this loving and safe learning environment, we have the privilege of teaching children about their Heavenly Father. We have the opportunity to share the stories of God's faithfulness, His incredible love, and His desire for a personal relationship with them. As we guide children through age-appropriate Bible lessons, worship, and prayer, we empower them to discover the depth of God's love and truth for themselves.

Our role in Kids Ministry extends beyond imparting knowledge. We have the responsibility to nurture children's spiritual growth and equip them with a solid foundation of faith. In doing so, we help them develop a lifelong relationship with their Heavenly Father and prepare them to impact the world for His glory.

Heavenly Father, we thank You for the privilege of welcoming children into our Kids Ministry. Help us to create a loving and safe learning environment where children can encounter Your love and truth. Give us wisdom in areas we need to grow and change in. Guide us in modeling Your love, grace, and kindness to every child we serve. Grant us the wisdom to establish boundaries and protocols that protect their well-being. May our ministry be a reflection of Your unconditional love, and may children experience Your presence in our midst. In Jesus' name, we pray. Amen.

Takeaway

Creating a loving and safe learning environment for children in Kids Ministry matters to God. As we welcome children in Jesus' name, we demonstrate our love for Him and reflect His love for them. Let us be intentional in cultivating an atmosphere of care, acceptance, and security where all children can learn about their Heavenly Father. Through our ministry, may children experience the transforming power of God's love and grow in their relationship with Him. IT MATTERS.

_____

_____

_____

_____

_____

_____

_____

_____

_____

THE BEST INVESTMENT
WE CAN MAKE IS IN THE
spiritual growth
OF OUR CHILDREN.

WEEK 4 : IT MATTERS TO GOD
Solid as a Rock: Building Kids' Faith on the Unshakable Truth of Scripture

"All Scripture is God-breathed and is useful for teaching, rebuking, correcting and training in righteousness, so that the servant of God may be thoroughly equipped for every good work."
2 Timothy 3:16-17

One of the core reasons why Kids Ministry matters to God is the vital role it plays in teaching children the truth and foundations of Scripture. In a world filled with conflicting messages, it is crucial that we ground children in the unchanging truth of God's Word.

In 2 Timothy 3:16-17, the apostle Paul affirms the divine inspiration and authority of Scripture. He emphasizes that every part of Scripture is God-breathed and carries immense value for teaching, rebuking, correcting, and training in righteousness. As children's ministry leaders and volunteers, we are responsible for imparting this truth to the next generation.

Teaching lessons based on the truth and foundations of Scripture is of utmost importance because it provides children with a solid spiritual grounding. The Bible is not just a collection of stories; it is God's revelation of Himself, His purposes, and His plan of redemption for humanity. When we teach children from Scripture, we introduce them to the living Word of God and equip them with the tools they need to navigate life with a godly perspective.

In a world that often distorts truth and promotes relativism, teaching children the unchanging truth of Scripture is a powerful antidote. This foundation is essentially giving kids a toolbox for life that they can use whenever needed. It instills in them a foundation of absolute truth that can guide their decisions, shape their values, and anchor their faith. It helps them develop discernment, enabling them to recognize and stand against the falsehoods that may seek to influence their lives.

Moreover, teaching biblical truths prepares children to face the challenges and trials they may encounter. The Scriptures provide timeless wisdom and guidance for every aspect of life. When children understand and internalize these truths, they are equipped to make godly choices, overcome obstacles, and live out their faith with confidence.

As we teach lessons based on the truth and foundations of Scripture, we must approach it with reverence and accuracy. It is essential to handle the Word of God with care, ensuring that we convey its intended message faithfully. We should pray for wisdom and rely on the Holy Spirit to guide our teaching, allowing the Scriptures to speak to the hearts of children in a way that is relevant and transformative. Our lessons each week should be "handles" to scripture for our kids to carry out of our class and apply in their own lives starting that very day.

Teaching children from the truth and foundations of Scripture is a sacred privilege. It is a divine partnership between God, His Word, and us as stewards of His truth. As we faithfully teach children, we participate in their spiritual formation and help them become "thoroughly equipped for every good work," as mentioned in 2 Timothy.

Heavenly Father, we thank You for the gift of Your Word. Help us to approach teaching children from the truth and foundations of Scripture with humility, reverence, and accuracy. Grant us wisdom as we convey Your truth in a way that captures their hearts and minds. May Your Word take root in their lives, transforming and equipping them for every good work. In Jesus' name, we pray. Amen.

Takeaway

Teaching lessons based on the truth and foundations of Scripture is a vital aspect of Kids Ministry. It provides children with a solid spiritual grounding, equips them to discern truth from falsehood, and prepares them to face life's challenges. As we faithfully teach children, let us remember the profound impact that the Word of God can have on their lives, shaping them into faithful followers of Christ. IT MATTERS.

_____

_____

_____

_____

_____

_____

_____

_____

CHILDREN'S MINISTRY
IS NOT JUST ABOUT
ENTERTAINING KIDS;
IT'S ABOUT

empowering

FUTURE LEADERS.

WEEK 5 : IT MATTERS TO GOD
Beyond Programming – Nurturing Discipleship

"These commandments that I give you today are to be on your hearts. Impress them on your children. Talk about them when you sit at home and when you walk along the road, when you lie down and when you get up."
Deuteronomy 6:6-7

Deuteronomy 6:6-7 is a powerful reminder of the importance of relationship and connection in nurturing faith. God instructed the Israelites to impress His commandments on their children continually—when sitting at home, walking along the road, lying down, and getting up. This passage reveals that discipleship is not limited to scheduled programming but involves a holistic approach that encompasses daily interactions and intentional conversations.

In Kids Ministry, building relationships is key to effective discipleship. It is through relationships that trust is established, hearts are opened, and the foundation for meaningful spiritual growth is laid. When we invest time and effort in developing connections with children, we create spaces for authenticity, vulnerability, and mentorship to flourish. Through genuine relationships, we can impart godly wisdom, provide guidance, and walk alongside children as they navigate their faith journey.

Discipleship is not confined to the church building; it happens throughout the week in various settings. It is in everyday moments, such as family meals, car rides, bedtime routines, and morning conversations, that discipleship opportunities arise. These are the times when we can engage children in discussions about faith, share personal stories of God's faithfulness, and encourage them to apply biblical truths to their daily lives. By integrating discipleship into the fabric of everyday life, we help children see that their relationship with God is not confined to a Sunday experience but permeates every aspect of their existence.

Fostering connection and discipleship beyond programming requires intentionality. It involves equipping parents and guardians to become primary spiritual influencers in their children's lives. By providing resources, support, and encouragement to families, we empower them to carry out discipleship practices at home. This partnership between the church and families strengthens children's spiritual foundation and reinforces the importance of faith in their daily lives.

As we engage in Kids Ministry, let us remember that discipleship is a lifelong journey. It is not a one-time event but a continuous process of growth and transformation. It requires our commitment, patience, and willingness to invest in the lives of children beyond the confines of programmed activities. Through intentional relationship-building and discipleship, we have the opportunity to shape the next generation of disciples who will impact the world for God's glory.

Heavenly Father, we thank You for the privilege of participating in Kids Ministry. Help us to embrace the call to discipleship and go beyond programming, nurturing relationships and connections that foster spiritual growth. Grant us wisdom to engage children in authentic conversations and to integrate discipleship into everyday moments. May our efforts in Kids Ministry be marked by intentionality and a deep desire to guide children in their walk with You. In Jesus' name, we pray. Amen.

Takeaway

Kids Ministry is more than just programming; it is about discipleship. By building relationships, fostering connection, and engaging in intentional discipleship throughout the week, we create spaces for spiritual growth and transformation. Let us be intentional in nurturing relationships with children and equipping families to carry out discipleship practices at home. Through our efforts, may children experience the joy of walking with God and grow into passionate disciples who impact the world for His glory. IT MATTERS.

_____

_____

_____

_____

_____

_____

_____

_____

IN CHILDREN'S MINISTRY,
WE PLANT THE

seeds of faith,

TRUSTING GOD
TO MAKE THEM GROW.

WEEK 6 : IT MATTERS TO GOD
Shaping Lives, Not Babysitting

"Train up a child in the way he should go;
even when he is old he will not depart from it."
Proverbs 22:6

Kids Ministry is far more than mere babysitting—it is a sacred calling to shape and mold lives. As children's pastors and leaders, we have the tremendous responsibility and privilege of guiding young hearts in their journey of faith.

Proverbs 22:6 presents an essential truth: we are called to "train up a child in the way he should go." This verse speaks of the profound impact our ministry can have on the lives of children. It challenges us to recognize that what we do in Kids Ministry goes beyond simply supervising and entertaining children—it involves intentional discipleship and shaping their futures.

As children's pastors and leaders, we are entrusted with the task of building a spiritual foundation in the lives of young ones. We have the privilege of imparting biblical truths, modeling godly character, and nurturing a love for Jesus in their hearts. Our role is not just to occupy their time but to invest in their eternal destinies.

Children are like sponges, eager to learn, grow, and absorb the world around them. They are impressionable and deeply influenced by the relationships and experiences they encounter. As we engage in Kids Ministry, we have the opportunity to shape their understanding of God, His Word, and the love of Jesus. We have the chance to help them develop a genuine and personal relationship with their Heavenly Father.

In our ministry, we are called to be more than caretakers or entertainers. We are called to be shepherds, mentors, and spiritual guides. We are responsible for creating an environment that fosters growth, discipleship, and a deep sense of belonging. We should seek to understand each child's unique needs, talents, abilities, and challenges, providing them with the support and encouragement they need to flourish.

Moreover, our ministry extends beyond the walls of the church. We have the opportunity to partner with parents, walking alongside them as they raise their children in the ways of the Lord. By providing resources, tools, and a supportive community, we empower families to reinforce the lessons learned in Kids Ministry and create a holistic spiritual environment for their children.

As we reflect on the importance of our call in Kids Ministry, let us remember that we are not merely babysitting; we are shaping lives. Every interaction, lesson taught, prayer offered, and act of love has the potential to impact a child's life trajectory. By faithfully fulfilling our calling, we participate in God's work of transformation, laying a solid foundation for future generations.

Heavenly Father, we thank You for the privilege of serving in Kids Ministry. Help us to recognize the profound impact we can have on the lives of children. Grant us wisdom, patience, and love as we shape and mold young hearts. May our ministry go beyond babysitting as we invest in the eternal destinies of the children entrusted to us. In Jesus' name, we pray. Amen.

Takeaway

Kids Ministry is a sacred calling to shape and mold lives, not merely provide childcare. As children's pastors and leaders, we have the opportunity to train children in the ways of the Lord, imparting biblical truths and modeling godly character. Let us approach our ministry with a deep sense of purpose, knowing that what we do today has the potential to impact the future. May we faithfully fulfill our calling to shape lives, leaving a lasting legacy for the glory of God. IT MATTERS.

_____

_____

_____

_____

_____

_____

_____

_____

CHILDREN'S MINISTRY IS THE

heartbeat

OF THE CHURCH,
NURTURING THE FAITH
OF THE NEXT GENERATION.

WEEK 7 : IT MATTERS TO GOD
Infectious Love: Nurturing Our Spiritual Walk in Kids Ministry

"Do your best to present yourself to God as one approved, a worker who does not need to be ashamed and who correctly handles the word of truth."
2 Timothy 2:15

In the realm of Kids Ministry, our spiritual health matters deeply to God. As children's pastors, leaders, and volunteers, we need to prioritize our spiritual walk and well-being. This is a make-it-or-break-it aspect of our success in influencing and our ability to stay faithful to our calling.

In 2 Timothy 2:15, the apostle Paul encourages Timothy to do his best to present himself to God as one approved, a worker who does not need to be ashamed and who correctly handles the word of truth. This verse emphasizes the significance of knowing and correctly handling the Word of God. As children's pastors and leaders, we have a responsibility to be well-grounded in the Scriptures before we can effectively teach them to others.

Nurturing our spiritual walk involves a commitment to knowing and studying the Word of God for ourselves and not just for lesson prep. By immersing ourselves in the Scriptures, we gain a deeper understanding of God's character, promises, and redemptive plan. This knowledge equips us to teach and guide children with accuracy and authority, ensuring that they receive the truth of God's Word.

However, it is not enough to possess head knowledge alone. Our spiritual walk extends beyond the intellectual realm. We must strive to apply the truths we learn and cultivate a vibrant and authentic relationship with Jesus. Our love for Jesus should be contagious—so contagious that it ignites a passion for Him in the hearts of the children we serve!

To nurture a contagious love for Jesus, we must prioritize our own spiritual growth. We need to be intentional about spending time in prayer, seeking God's presence, and allowing Him to transform our hearts. As we deepen our personal relationship with Jesus, our love and enthusiasm for Him become evident to those around us. Children observe and absorb our attitudes, actions, and devotion, and it impacts their own spiritual journey. Our excitement about Jesus becomes their excitement about Jesus.

Moreover, a strong spiritual walk and prayer life enable us to lead with strength and grace. Kids Ministry can be demanding and challenging, requiring wisdom, patience, and endurance. When we are spiritually nourished and grounded, we can draw from the wellspring of God's strength and wisdom to guide and minister to children effectively.

As we prioritize our own spiritual health, we become vessels of God's love and truth to the children we serve. Our contagious love for Jesus inspires and empowers them to develop their own personal relationship with Him. Children are drawn to authenticity and passion, and when they witness our genuine love for Jesus, it sparks a desire within them to know Him more deeply.

Dear Heavenly Father, we thank You for the privilege of serving in Kids Ministry. Help us to prioritize our own spiritual health and well-being. Strengthen our love for Jesus, and may it be contagious to all those we serve. Grant us the wisdom to correctly handle Your Word and the grace to lead with strength and grace. May our lives reflect a genuine and vibrant relationship with Jesus, inspiring children to seek Him wholeheartedly. In Jesus' name, we pray. Amen.

Takeaway

As children's pastors and leaders, we need to take care of ourselves spiritually to effectively lead in Kids Ministry. By knowing and correctly handling the Word of God, being strong in our spiritual walk, and nurturing a contagious love for Jesus, we can inspire and empower children to develop their own personal relationships with Him. Let us prioritize our spiritual health, allowing God to work in and through us to impact the lives of the children entrusted to our care. IT MATTERS.

_____

_____

_____

_____

_____

_____

_____

_____

CHILDREN'S MINISTRY IS A
JOURNEY OF FAITH WHERE

God's grace

AND LOVE MEET
YOUNG HEARTS.

WEEK 8 : IT MATTERS TO GOD
Divine Support for a Heavenly Task

"He gives strength to the weary and increases the power of the weak."
Isaiah 40:29

Children's Ministry is a calling that requires reliance on God's strength. As leaders, teachers, and volunteers in Kids Ministry, we understand that our own abilities are limited, but through God's strength, we can accomplish the great things He has called all of us to.

Isaiah 40:29 reminds us of the promise that God gives strength to the weary and increases the power of the weak. In the context of Children's Ministry, where the demands can be great and the challenges numerous, we need to rely on God's strength to sustain us and empower us to fulfill His calling.

In the journey of Children's Ministry, we encounter weariness and exhaustion. There are moments when we may feel overwhelmed by the responsibilities, the needs of the children, or the weight of the spiritual battles we face. However, we can turn to God, the ultimate source of strength in these moments. His presence and power can renew and rejuvenate us, enabling us to continue serving with passion and effectiveness.

When we lean on God's strength, we acknowledge our dependence on Him. We recognize that our abilities and resources are limited, but His power knows no bounds. As we surrender our weaknesses and limitations to Him, we open ourselves to experience His supernatural strength at work in and through us.

Furthermore, leaning on God's strength is an act of humility. It requires acknowledging that we are not self-sufficient but rather reliant on God for every aspect of our ministry. It is a humbling reminder that Children's Ministry is not about our abilities or achievements but about being vessels through which God's love, truth, and power can flow.

As we lean on God's strength, we also trust Him as our provider. Children's Ministry often requires creativity, resources, and wisdom beyond our own capacity. Whether it is materials for teaching, volunteers to assist, or guidance in challenging situations, we can trust that God will provide all that we need. He is the faithful provider who equips and sustains us in this important work.

Moreover, relying on God's strength in Children's Ministry enables us to bear lasting fruit. When we operate in our own strength, we may see temporary results, but when we depend on God, the impact goes beyond what we can imagine. His power can transform lives, shape destinies, and bring about eternal change in the hearts of children.

In the challenges and demands of Children's Ministry, let us intentionally lean on God's strength. Let us seek Him in prayer, rely on His guidance, and trust in His provision. As we do so, we will witness His power at work, enabling us to fulfill His calling with excellence and impacting the lives of children for His glory.

Heavenly Father, we thank You for the privilege of serving in the Children's Ministry. We acknowledge our need for Your strength and provision. Help us to lean on You in every aspect of our ministry. Renew our strength when we are weary, empower us when we feel weak, and guide us with Your wisdom. May Your power flow through us, transforming lives and bringing glory to Your name. In Jesus' name, we pray. Amen.

Takeaway

In Children's Ministry, it is essential to lean on God's strength. By acknowledging our dependence on Him, we open ourselves to experience His power at work in and through us. As we trust in His provision and rely on His guidance, we will see a lasting impact in the lives of children. Let us lean on God's strength, knowing that with Him, all things are possible in the important work of Children's Ministry. IT MATTERS.

_____

_____

_____

_____

_____

_____

_____

_____

KIDS ARE NOT JUST
THE CHURCH OF TOMORROW;
THEY ARE THE
church of today.

WEEK 9 : IT MATTERS TO GOD
Promises for Today and Tomorrow

"For no matter how many promises God has made, they are 'Yes' in Christ. And so through him, the 'Amen' is spoken by us to the glory of God."
2 Corinthians 1:20

Kids Ministry holds immense importance to God because His promises also extend to children. In this devotional, we will explore the significance of Kids Ministry in relation to God's promises.

The Bible is brimming with promises from God, declarations of His love, provision, guidance, and faithfulness. These promises are not limited to adults alone but also to children. Kids Ministry plays a vital role in helping children understand and apply these promises to their lives, even from a young age.

In 2 Corinthians 1:20, Paul assures us that all of God's promises find their fulfillment in Christ. Through Jesus, we have access to the abundance of God's promises, and we can speak the "Amen," affirming their truth and relevance in our lives. This truth is especially powerful when we help children understand and embrace it.

Children in Kids Ministry can begin to stand on God's promises even now. They can experience His love, protection, and provision firsthand. As we teach and reinforce these promises, children gain confidence in God's faithfulness and learn to trust Him in every aspect of their lives.

When children grasp the promises of God, it anchors their faith and provides a solid foundation for their relationship with Him. They learn to view the challenges they face through the lens of God's promises rather than the circumstances surrounding them. Promises such as "I am with you always" (Matthew 28:20) and "I will never leave you nor forsake you" (Hebrews 13:5) become their source of strength and courage.

Kids Ministry is a nurturing ground where children can discover and internalize the promises of God. We have the privilege of teaching them these promises and helping them develop a personal connection with each one. We can share stories of how God has been faithful throughout history and in our own lives, building their faith and trust in His promises.

Furthermore, as children learn to stand on God's promises, they develop a deep-rooted hope that carries them through their lifetime. These promises become an anchor for their souls, providing comfort, guidance, and assurance in the midst of life's uncertainties. They learn to navigate challenges, make wise choices, and find peace in knowing that God's promises are unchanging and true.

As we impart God's promises in Children's Ministry, we empower children to walk in the fullness of their identity as beloved children of God. We help them understand that they are heirs to His promises, entitled to His blessings, and recipients of His unending love. By nurturing their faith in God's promises, we lay a firm foundation for a lifetime of walking in His truth.:

Heavenly Father, we thank You for the abundance of promises found in Your Word. Help us to impart these promises to the children we serve in Kids Ministry. May they grasp the truth of Your faithfulness and learn to stand on Your promises with unwavering trust. Anchor their faith in Your Word, and may they experience the fullness of Your blessings throughout their lives. In Jesus' name, we pray. Amen.

Takeaway

Kids Ministry is significant to God because His promises extend to children as well. By teaching and reinforcing these promises, we anchor children's faith in God's truth and empower them to stand on His Word. As children learn to embrace God's promises from a young age, they develop a foundation of trust and hope that will guide them throughout their lives. Let us nurture their faith and help them experience the fullness of God's blessings through His promises. IT MATTERS.

_____

_____

_____

_____

_____

_____

_____

_____

IN CHILDREN'S MINISTRY,
WE HAVE THE OPPORTUNITY TO
shape the future
ONE CHILD AT A TIME.

WEEK 10 : IT MATTERS TO THE CHURCH
Little Giants of Faith: Unleashing the Church of Today through Kids Ministry

"Don't let anyone look down on you because you are young, but set an example for the believers in speech, in conduct, in love, in faith and in purity."
1 Timothy 4:12

Kids Ministry holds significant importance to the church because children are not just the future of the church; they are the church of today.

1 Timothy 4:12 reminds us that we should not underestimate the capabilities and significance of children in the church. Paul exhorts young Timothy not to allow anyone to look down on him because he is young. This verse highlights the truth that children have a vital role to play in the body of Christ, serving as examples for believers in various aspects of life.

Children possess unique gifts, perspectives, and abilities that can make a powerful impact on the church community. They have a genuine faith, a contagious love for Jesus, and a pure zeal for sharing His love with others. Kids Ministry plays a crucial role in nurturing and equipping children to serve, lead, and be missionaries in their spheres of influence.

Children are not limited by their age when it comes to serving within the church. They can actively participate in worship, prayer, and acts of service alongside adults. Their energy, enthusiasm, and fresh perspectives infuse new life into the church community. By involving children in various ministries and encouraging their participation, we create a vibrant and intergenerational church environment.

Moreover, children have the ability to lead and influence their peers and even adults. They can set an example for others in their speech, conduct, love, faith, and purity. Their genuine faith and childlike trust in God can inspire adults to rekindle their own faith and develop a deeper relationship with Jesus. Children have a unique way of drawing people to Christ through their innocent and authentic expressions of love, compassion, and obedience.

Kids Ministry empowers children to be missionaries to their friends and relatives. Children have natural connections and relationships within their communities, schools, and neighborhoods. They can be effective ambassadors of God's love by sharing their faith, inviting others to church, and demonstrating Christ's teachings through their actions. Their childlike faith and uncomplicated approach to sharing the gospel can touch hearts and lead others to experience the transforming power of Jesus.

The church of today needs the active involvement of children. Their presence brings joy, energy, and fresh perspectives that enhance the unity and diversity of the body of Christ. When we invest in Kids Ministry, we create an environment where children are valued, encouraged, and equipped to fulfill their God-given potential as active members of the church community.

Heavenly Father, we thank You for the children in our midst who are part of the church of today. Help us to recognize and value their unique contributions. Empower them to serve, lead, and be missionaries in their spheres of influence. May we create a welcoming and inclusive environment where children can actively participate and be examples to believers of all ages. In Jesus' name, we pray. Amen.

Takeaway

Kids Ministry matters to the church because children are not just the future; they are the church of today. When we empower children to serve, lead, and be missionaries, we unleash their God-given potential to make a profound impact within the church community and beyond. Let us value and nurture the active involvement of children, recognizing their unique contributions and fostering an intergenerational church environment filled with love, faith, and joy. IT MATTERS.

_____

_____

_____

_____

_____

_____

_____

_____

CHILDREN'S MINISTRY
IS A PLACE WHERE
little feet
FIND A PATH TO
FOLLOW JESUS.

WEEK 11 : IT MATTERS TO THE CHURCH
Raising Faith's Architects: Kids Ministry and the Future of the Church

"Start children off on the way they should go,
and even when they are old they will not turn from it."
Proverbs 22:6

Kids Ministry holds a critical role in shaping the future of the church. As we invest in children's spiritual growth and development, we are nurturing and equipping the architects of faith who will lead the church in the years to come.

Children are not only the future of the church but also the key to its continued growth and impact. Their hearts are fertile ground, ready to receive and embrace the teachings of the gospel. By investing in Kids Ministry, we are investing in the spiritual foundation of the next generation of believers.

Just as architects lay the foundation and design the structure of a building, Kids Ministry serves as a catalyst for cultivating the faith of children. The lessons, experiences, and relationships they encounter in Kids Ministry shape the framework upon which their faith will be built. We have the privilege of guiding them, providing a solid foundation in God's Word, and helping them develop a personal relationship with Jesus.

Kids Ministry is a place where children can encounter the living God and experience His transformative power. It is where seeds of faith are planted, watered, and nurtured. Through engaging lessons, worship, prayer, and meaningful connections with leaders and peers, children can begin to understand the depth of God's love and His redemptive plan for their lives.

As we pour into children in Kids Ministry, we have the opportunity to equip them with the tools they need to navigate the challenges of life with a firm faith in Christ. We teach them the truths of Scripture, instilling in them a biblical worldview that will guide their decisions and shape their values. By teaching them to seek God's wisdom, listen to His voice, and rely on His strength, we empower them to be effective witnesses for Christ in their families, schools, and communities.

Kids Ministry also provides a supportive environment for children to grow in their faith alongside their peers. Through fellowship, worship, and shared experiences, children build relationships that strengthen and encourage them in their journey. These connections foster accountability and create a sense of belonging, reminding them that they are not alone in their pursuit of faith.

Moreover, the Kids Ministry serves as a training ground for leadership development. As we encourage children to step out of their comfort zones, serve others, and use their unique gifts and talents, we empower them to become leaders who will impact their generation and beyond. By providing opportunities for them to lead in age-appropriate ways, we instill in them a sense of responsibility and purpose within the church.

In the hands of God, children can become powerful agents of change, advancing His kingdom and bringing hope to the world. By investing in Kids Ministry, we invest in the future of the church. We plant seeds of faith that will grow and flourish, shaping generations to come. Let us raise up the architects of faith, instilling in them a deep love for God, a passion for His Word, and a desire to live out their faith boldly.

Heavenly Father, we thank You for the privilege of investing in the future of the church through Kids Ministry. Help us to raise up the architects of faith, children who will impact their world for Your glory. Guide us as we nurture their faith, instill in them a love for Your Word, and empower them to be leaders in their generation. May they be filled with passion and boldness to share Your love and truth with others. In Jesus' name, we pray. Amen.

Takeaway

Kids Ministry plays a vital role in shaping the future of the church. By investing in children's spiritual growth and development, we equip them as architects of faith, laying a firm foundation and empowering them to impact their generation and beyond. Let us embrace the opportunity to nurture their faith, instill biblical values, and provide them with a supportive community where they can grow, lead, and become agents of change. Together, we are building a strong and vibrant future for the church. IT MATTERS.

_____

_____

_____

_____

_____

_____

_____

_____

KIDS ARE NOT INTERRUPTIONS; THEY ARE

divine appointments.

WEEK 12 : IT MATTERS
TO THE CHURCH
The Littlest People Bring the Greatest Joy

"Children are a heritage from the Lord, offspring a reward from him."
Psalm 127:3

Children's Ministry holds immense importance to the church because it would lack the vibrant joy and contagious energy they bring without kids.

Psalm 127:3 reminds us that children are a heritage from the Lord, a reward from Him. This verse encapsulates the truth that children are not just passive members of the church but valuable contributors who bring joy, energy, and a sense of wonder to the body of Christ.

Children have a remarkable ability to bring joy to the church community. Their infectious laughter, boundless enthusiasm, and genuine love for God can brighten the atmosphere and uplift the spirits of those around them. In their presence, we are reminded of the simple joys of life and the beauty of childlike faith.

Moreover, children's energy infuses the church with vitality and excitement. They possess an eagerness to learn, explore, and engage in various church activities. Their enthusiasm spills over into worship, prayer, and fellowship, inspiring others to approach their faith with renewed passion and zeal. Through their unreserved engagement, they encourage the church to be actively involved in every aspect of ministry.

Children's perspectives and questions challenge and inspire the church body to embrace childlike curiosity and humility. Their innocent and honest inquiries prompt us to explore our own understanding of faith and deepen our relationship with God. As we journey alongside them, we rediscover the wonder of God's creation and the awe-inspiring truths found in His Word.

Kids Ministry plays a vital role in nurturing the joy and energy that children bring to the church. It provides a space where their unique qualities are celebrated and their voices are heard and valued. By offering age-appropriate teachings, engaging activities, and opportunities for children to participate, Kids Ministry creates an environment where children can thrive, develop their gifts, and grow in their relationship with Jesus.

As the church embraces children, we create a sense of belonging and build intergenerational connections. We foster relationships where children are mentored, loved, and nurtured by adults and where adults are inspired, encouraged, and humbled by children. Together, we form a tapestry of diverse backgrounds, ages, and experiences that reflects the beautiful diversity of God's kingdom.

The presence of children in the church reminds us of the importance of investing in the next generation. By equipping them with a solid foundation in the Word, teaching them about the love and grace of Jesus, and modeling a life devoted to Him, we empower children to carry the torch of faith and continue the work of the church. Their active involvement today prepares them to be leaders, influencers, and ambassadors of Christ in the future.

Heavenly Father, we thank You for the gift of children in the church. Help us to recognize and appreciate the unique contributions they bring. May we create a nurturing environment where they can grow, thrive, and be filled with joy and energy. Guide us as we invest in Kids Ministry, empowering children to become faithful followers of Jesus and passionate members of the church. In Jesus' name, we pray. Amen.

Takeaway

Children's Ministry matters to the church because children are not just passive members; they infuse the body of Christ with joy and energy. By creating a space where children are celebrated, engaged, and mentored, we cultivate a vibrant and dynamic church community. Let us embrace the joy and energy children bring, recognizing their value and investing in their spiritual growth. Together, we can build a church that reflects the beauty of God's kingdom and nurtures the faith of future generations. IT MATTERS.

_____

_____

_____

_____

_____

_____

_____

_____

CHILDREN'S MINISTRY IS LIKE
A PUZZLE,
FITTING THE PIECES OF
God's Word
INTO YOUNG HEARTS.

WEEK 13 : IT MATTERS TO THE CHURCH

United in Purpose: The Importance of a Children's Pastor in the Kidmin Community

As iron sharpens iron, so one person sharpens another."
Proverbs 27:17

In the context of Children's Ministry, the role of a Children's Pastor holds immense significance. They serve as vital connectors, mentors, and leaders within the Kidmin community.

Children's Ministry thrives when there is strong leadership and a sense of unity within the Kidmin community. The role of a Children's Pastor is crucial in fostering a collective spirit, creating a space where team members can link arms and work together towards a common purpose. Like the analogy of iron sharpening iron, a Children's Pastor plays a vital role in sharpening and encouraging the team members, enhancing their effectiveness in ministry.

As a Children's Pastor, you serve as a connector, bringing together individuals with diverse gifts, talents, and experiences for the purpose of ministering to children. Your role is not only to provide guidance and direction but also to empower and equip the team. Just as iron sharpens iron, you sharpen the team members, encouraging them to grow, learn, and excel in their areas of service.

Unity among the Kidmin team is crucial in fulfilling the important task that God has called us to. When we are united in purpose and commitment, we can maximize our impact and effectively minister to children and families. As a Children's Pastor, you have the opportunity to foster this unity, creating an environment where team members feel valued, supported, and connected to a greater vision.

The collaborative nature of Children's Ministry calls for humility, recognizing that we need one another's strengths, perspectives, and expertise. No one person can do it all, but together, as a team, we can create a holistic and impactful ministry. When team members link arms, their individual strengths and gifts complement one another, resulting in a more comprehensive and transformative ministry experience for children.

As a Kidmin leader, you have the privilege of leading by example, cultivating a culture of collaboration and unity within the Kidmin community. Encourage team members to share their ideas, insights, and creativity. Provide opportunities for open dialogue, mutual learning, and collective problem-solving. When team members feel heard, valued, and part of a larger mission, their passion and dedication to the Children's Ministry are deepened.

Just as iron sharpens iron, the Kidmin team sharpens one another through shared experiences, encouragement, and accountability. As a Children's Pastor, you have the responsibility to create opportunities for team members to grow spiritually, professionally, and personally. Foster a continuous learning and development culture, providing resources, training, and mentoring to help team members sharpen their skills and deepen their faith.

In this collaborative journey, it is essential to remember that our ultimate source of strength and guidance is God. As we link arms and work together, let us constantly seek His wisdom, guidance, and empowerment. In His presence, we find unity, strength, and inspiration to fulfill the important task of the Children's Ministry.

Heavenly Father, we thank You for the gift of the team and the calling to Children's Ministry. Help us to embrace our roles as Children's Pastors, connectors, and leaders within the Kidmin community. May we foster a spirit of unity, collaboration, and mutual support among the team members. Equip us to sharpen one another, empowering each individual to excel in their areas of service. Guide us in seeking Your wisdom and leading as we work together for the glory of Your name. In Jesus' name, we pray. Amen.

Takeaway

A Children's Pastor plays a vital role in fostering unity, collaboration, and mutual support within the Kidmin community. Like iron sharpening iron, they encourage team members to grow, excel, and fulfill their calling in Children's Ministry. Together, as a team, we can create a transformative ministry experience for children and families. Let us embrace our roles as connectors and leaders, linking arms and working together to fulfill the important task that God has called us to. IT MATTERS.

_____

_____

_____

_____

_____

_____

_____

_____

_____

IN CHILDREN'S MINISTRY,
WE ARE BUILDING BRIDGES
to eternity.

WEEK 14 : IT MATTERS TO THE CHURCH
Championing Our Pastors: Children's Pastors as Sidekicks with Superpowers

"Obey your leaders and submit to them, for they are keeping watch over your souls, as those who will have to give an account. Let them do this with joy and not with groaning, for that would be of no advantage to you."
Hebrews 13:17

In the tapestry of the church, the role of a Children's Pastor is of immense importance. Children's Pastors serve as a valuable support system to the overall pastoral leadership.

As a Children's Pastor, you have the unique privilege of supporting and blessing the pastors of the church through your dedicated service in Children's Ministry. You are an essential part of the team that helps fulfill the vision and mission of the church. Your role extends beyond ministering to children; it involves actively supporting the goals and ideas of the pastoral leadership.

Hebrews 13:17 urges us to obey and submit to our leaders, recognizing that they are watching our souls. The pastors bear the weight of spiritual accountability and the responsibility of guiding the flock. As a Children's Pastor, your role is to align your ministry with the overarching vision of the church and support the pastors' goals and ideas. This collaboration creates a harmonious environment where the church can flourish.

Sometimes, supporting our pastors' goals and ideas may present challenges or require personal sacrifice. It may require us to step out of our comfort zones, adapt to changes, or stretch beyond our perceived limitations. Yet, serving with humility and a willingness to align our ministry with the greater vision allows us to create a strong and unified church community.

Children's Ministry holds immense importance in the church because it impacts the lives of the youngest members and shapes the future of the church. As a Children's Pastor, you have the privilege of nurturing the faith of the next generation, ensuring that they are rooted in the love and teachings of Jesus. This invaluable work brings joy to the pastors' hearts, knowing that the children are being taught about Jesus and experiencing true life change.

By faithfully serving in Children's Ministry, you provide pastors with the assurance that the church is investing in the spiritual growth and development of every generation. You bless them with the knowledge that the church is actively cultivating a vibrant and enduring community of faith. The impact of Children's Ministry reaches beyond the children themselves; it influences families, impacts the church body, and shapes the culture of the entire congregation.

As a Children's Pastor, it is essential to approach your role with a humble and teachable spirit. Recognize that you are part of a larger team working towards a common goal. Seek opportunities to collaborate with the pastoral leadership, valuing their insights, guidance, and wisdom. By doing so, you create an environment where mutual support and respect thrive, and the entire church body is strengthened.

Heavenly Father, we thank You for the pastors and leaders in the church who diligently watch over our souls. As Children's Pastors, help us to support and bless them through our dedicated service. May we align our ministry with the vision and goals of the church, serving with humility and a teachable spirit. Grant us wisdom and discernment to nurture the faith of the next generation and bring joy to the hearts of our pastors. In Jesus' name, we pray. Amen.

Takeaway

As Children's Pastors, we have the privilege of supporting and blessing the pastors of the church through our dedicated service. By aligning our ministry with their goals and ideas, we contribute to a harmonious and unified church community. Children's Ministry plays a vital role in nurturing the faith of the next generation, bringing joy to the hearts of pastors as they witness the spiritual growth and transformation happening in each generation. Let us serve with humility, embracing our role as supporters and collaborators in fulfilling the vision and mission of the church. IT MATTERS.

_____

_____

_____

_____

_____

_____

_____

_____

CHILDREN'S MINISTRY
IS WHERE
big faith
BEGINS WITH LITTLE STEPS.

WEEK 15 : IT MATTERS TO THE CHURCH

Generations United: Kidmin's Role in Building Intergenerational Community

"One generation shall commend your works to another,
and shall declare your mighty acts."
Psalm 145:4

Kidmin matters greatly because it fosters intergenerational relationships within the church. It brings together children, parents, and older adults, creating a beautiful tapestry of community across different age groups.

Psalm 145:4 beautifully captures the essence of intergenerational connections within the church. It emphasizes the role of one generation commending God's works to another, declaring His mighty acts. In the context of Kidmin, this verse speaks to the importance of fostering relationships and sharing the faith journey across different age groups.

Children's Ministry serves as a catalyst for intergenerational connections within the church. It provides a space for children, parents, and older adults to come together, learn from one another, and grow in their faith together. Through shared experiences, collaborative activities, and meaningful interactions, Kidmin nurtures a sense of community that transcends generational boundaries.

Children benefit significantly from intergenerational relationships. They are shaped not only by their peers but also by the wisdom, love, and mentorship of older adults in the church. The presence of mature believers provides guidance, spiritual nurturing, and role models for children to look up to. As they witness the faith in action, children are inspired to develop their own vibrant relationship with God.

Parents also find support and encouragement through intergenerational connections in Kidmin. They can learn from seasoned parents who have walked the journey before them, gaining insights, wisdom, and practical advice. The shared experiences create a bond that helps parents navigate the joys and challenges of raising children in the faith.

Furthermore, older adults find purpose and fulfillment in engaging with children in the church. They have the opportunity to pass on their faith, life experiences, and wisdom to the younger generation. Through their involvement in Kidmin, they become spiritual mentors, encouragers, and prayer warriors for the children and families. Their presence brings stability, depth, and a sense of continuity to the church community.

Intergenerational connections in Kidmin enrich the worship experience of the entire church. As children participate in worship alongside their parents and older adults, they learn the importance of corporate worship and the significance of praising God as a community. The diverse expressions of worship, prayers, and testimonies from different generations create a tapestry of worship that reflects the beauty and diversity of God's family.

Additionally, intergenerational relationships foster fellowship and a sense of belonging within the church. When children, parents, and older adults come together in Kidmin activities, they form bonds that extend beyond age. They create a safe and nurturing environment where everyone feels valued and accepted. This sense of belonging strengthens the fabric of the church, building a community that supports, encourages, and challenges one another in their faith journeys.

In Kidmin, we have the opportunity to create intentional spaces for intergenerational interactions. Whether it is through family events, mentorship programs, or service opportunities, we can foster connections that unite different generations in the pursuit of a deeper relationship with God. When we prioritize intergenerational relationships, we reflect God's desire for unity and community within His church.

Heavenly Father, we thank You for the gift of intergenerational connections within the church. Help us to prioritize and foster relationships across different age groups through Kidmin. May we learn from one another, grow together in faith, and support each other's spiritual journeys. Strengthen our sense of community and unity as we commend Your works from one generation to another. In Jesus' name, we pray. Amen.

Takeaway

Kidmin matters greatly because it nurtures intergenerational connections within the church. It brings children, parents, and older adults together, creating a sense of community that enriches worship, fellowship, and spiritual vitality. By fostering intentional relationships across generations, we create spaces where faith is shared, wisdom is passed down, and unity is celebrated. Let us embrace the beauty of intergenerational connections in Kidmin, knowing that as one generation commends God's works to another, we build a stronger and more vibrant church community. IT MATTERS.

_____

_____

_____

_____

_____

_____

_____

_____

_____

IN CHILDREN'S MINISTRY,
WE MAY NOT SEE
THE FRUIT NOW,
BUT GOD IS WORKING
in every heart.

WEEK 16 : IT MATTERS
TO THE CHURCH
Beyond Sunday School: Kidmin's Role in Reaching Families and Communities

"Go therefore and make disciples of all nations, baptizing them in the name of the Father and of the Son and of the Holy Spirit, teaching them to observe all that I have commanded you. And behold, I am with you always, to the end of the age."
Matthew 28:19-20

Kidmin matters greatly because it plays a vital role in church growth and outreach efforts. When children experience a welcoming and engaging children's ministry, they become catalysts for inviting their friends and families to church.

Matthew 28:19-20, often referred to as the Great Commission, encompasses the core mission of the church. As we go forth to make disciples, we are called to baptize and teach, empowering others to observe all that Jesus commanded. Kidmin becomes a vital bridge to fulfilling this commission, reaching not only children but also their families and communities.

Children's Ministry has the power to create a welcoming and engaging environment for children where they can encounter the love of Jesus and grow in their faith. When children experience the transformative power of God's Word and the love of the church community, they become enthusiastic participants in inviting their friends, classmates, and families to join them in this journey.

Children naturally have a heart for outreach. Their innocence, enthusiasm, and authenticity make them powerful messengers of God's love. When they are touched by the grace of Jesus in Kidmin, they carry that love into their homes, schools, and neighborhoods. Their excitement becomes contagious, drawing others to experience the joy and transformation found in a relationship with Christ.

Through Kidmin, we create opportunities for children to engage with the gospel and be discipled in their faith. As they grow in their understanding and commitment to Jesus, they become ambassadors for the church's mission. Their active participation and involvement in children's ministry events, service projects, and outreach initiatives contribute to the growth of the church and the expansion of its reach.

Children's Ministry serves as a gateway for reaching new families and communities with the message of God's love. When families witness the impact of Kidmin on their children's lives, they are often inspired to explore their own faith journey and engage in the life of the church. By investing in children's ministry, the church becomes a welcoming and inviting space for families to encounter Christ together.

Moreover, children's ministry acts as a nurturing ground for future generations of believers and leaders. As children grow in their faith through Kidmin, they are equipped to become faithful disciples who carry the torch of the gospel into the world. By empowering children to be active participants in the mission of the church, we ensure the growth and continuity of the church for generations to come.

In the spirit of the Great Commission, Kidmin invites us to go beyond the walls of the church and into the lives of families, communities, and nations. By intentionally creating a welcoming, engaging, and transformative children's ministry, we become agents of change, bridging the gap between the church and the world. We embrace the opportunity to make disciples, not only among children but also among families, as we strive to fulfill God's calling.

Heavenly Father, we thank You for the privilege of serving in Kidmin and being part of Your mission to make disciples. Guide us as we create welcoming and engaging environments for children to encounter You. Empower us to reach new families and communities with the message of Your love. May Kidmin be a bridge that leads others to experience the transformation found in a relationship with Jesus. In His name, we pray. Amen.

Takeaway

Kidmin plays a vital role in church growth and outreach efforts. By creating welcoming and engaging children's ministry experiences, we empower children to become ambassadors of God's love and invite others to encounter Jesus. As we go forth, bridging the gap between the church and the world, we fulfill the Great Commission and expand the church's reach. Let us embrace the privilege of serving in Kidmin, knowing that through it, we have the opportunity to make a lasting impact for the Kingdom of God. IT MATTERS.

_____

_____

_____

_____

_____

_____

_____

_____

CHILDREN'S MINISTRY
IS A CLASSROOM OF
compassion and love.

WEEK 17 : IT MATTERS TO THE CHURCH
The Sound of Joy: Kids in Worship and the Celebration They Bring

"Make a joyful noise to the Lord, all the earth! Serve the Lord with gladness!
Come into his presence with singing!"
Psalm 100:1-2

Kidmin matters greatly because it adds an element of vibrancy and joy to worship services. The presence of children in the church brings energy, enthusiasm, and a childlike faith that Jesus praised.

Children have a unique ability to infuse worship services with a sense of energy, enthusiasm, and joy. Their presence and participation in singing, prayer, and other elements of worship create an atmosphere that is contagious and inspiring. As we observe their childlike faith, we are reminded of the words in Psalm 100:1-2, which urge us to make a joyful noise to the Lord, serving Him with gladness and coming into His presence with singing.

Children bring a refreshing perspective to worship. Their sincerity, spontaneity, and uninhibited praise remind us to approach God with childlike wonder and awe. Their genuine excitement and passion for God's presence encourage the rest of the congregation to engage more deeply in worship. The joy that emanates from their hearts becomes a catalyst for collective celebration and praise.

Furthermore, children's participation in singing uplifts the entire worship experience. Their voices, though small, carry an authenticity and purity that touches the hearts of those around them. When children sing with all their might, they demonstrate a simple yet powerful expression of love for God. Their voices blend with those of the adults, creating a harmonious symphony of worship that glorifies God and stirs the soul.

Children also bring a sense of unity to the church as they join in prayer. Their innocent and heartfelt prayers remind us of the simplicity and trust that characterize a child's relationship with their Heavenly Father. Their prayers carry a genuine belief in the power of God and a deep desire to connect with Him. When children pray, it encourages the adults to approach God with a similar level of trust and dependency.

Kidmin serves as a catalyst for cultivating a culture of celebration in the church. Children's infectious joy and enthusiasm remind us that worship is not just a duty but a privilege and a delight. Their uninhibited dance, clapping, and expressions of praise inspire others to let go of inhibitions and worship God with abandon. The church is reminded of the call to rejoice and make a joyful noise to the Lord.

Moreover, Kidmin encourages a multi-generational worship experience. When children actively participate in worship, they become an integral part of the larger church community. As the congregation witnesses children engaging in worship, it fosters a sense of belonging and inclusivity. Children are no longer viewed as spectators but as valuable contributors to the worship service, strengthening the unity and diversity within the church.

As we embrace the childlike spirit in worship, we create an environment where everyone can experience the transformative power of God's presence. The vibrant worship experience that results from children's participation uplifts the entire congregation, deepening their connection with God and fostering a greater sense of community.

Heavenly Father, we thank You for the gift of children and their presence in the church. Help us to embrace their childlike spirit in worship, experiencing the joy and vibrancy they bring. May their participation in singing, prayer, and other elements of worship inspire us to approach You with childlike faith and exuberance. Let our worship be a celebration of Your goodness and a reflection of the childlike trust we have in You. In Jesus' name, we pray. Amen.

Takeaway

Kidmin matters greatly in fostering vibrant worship experiences in the church. The presence and participation of children add energy, enthusiasm, and joy to worship services. As we observe their childlike faith, we are reminded of the call to make a joyful noise to the Lord, serving Him with gladness and coming into His presence with singing. Children's voices, prayers, and expressions of praise contribute to a lively and celebratory atmosphere, inspiring the entire congregation to worship God with authenticity and joy. Let us embrace the childlike spirit in worship, cultivating a vibrant and transformative worship experience for all. IT MATTERS.

_____

_____

_____

_____

_____

_____

_____

_____

KIDS ARE NOT JUST LISTENERS;
THEY ARE THE FUTURE

storytellers

OF GOD'S LOVE.

WEEK 18 : IT MATTERS TO THE FAMILY
Raising Warriors of Truth: The Role of Kidmin in Equipping Families

"If we are thrown into the blazing furnace, the God we serve is able to deliver us from it, and he will deliver us from Your Majesty's hand. But even if he does not, we want you to know, Your Majesty, that we will not serve your gods or worship the image of gold you have set up."
Daniel 3:17-18

Kidmin matters greatly to the family because it provides a foundation of truth and the power of the gospel amidst the secular influences of church and culture. In today's world, families face numerous challenges and pressures that can lead them astray from God's Word.

The story of Shadrach, Meshach, and Abednego in the book of Daniel provides a powerful example of unwavering faith in the face of secular influences. King Nebuchadnezzar erected a golden statue and commanded everyone to worship it. However, these three young men refused to bow down to the idol, standing firm in their allegiance to the one true God. They declared their faith in the God who is able to deliver them from the fiery furnace, but even if He chose not to, they would not compromise their devotion.

Similarly, in today's culture, families are bombarded with secular influences that challenge their faith and values. The media, popular culture, and societal pressures can easily steer families away from God's Word. However, Kidmin plays a vital role in equipping families with the truth of the Scriptures, reminding them of the power of the gospel, and strengthening their faith to resist these influences.

Through Kidmin, children and families learn biblical truths that anchor their lives in God's Word. The stories, teachings, and lessons from the Bible serve as a compass, guiding families through the complexities of life. In a world where truth is often distorted or relativized, Kidmin presents families with the unchanging and trustworthy Word of God.

Moreover, Kidmin nurtures a community of believers where families can find support, encouragement, and fellowship. This community serves as a safe haven for families to discuss challenges, seek guidance, and pray together. The shared experiences, testimonies, and genuine care for one another create a strong network of support that helps families navigate the secular influences of church and culture.

In the story of Shadrach, Meshach, and Abednego, we see their unwavering commitment to God's truth, regardless of the consequences. They recognized that their allegiance belonged to God alone, and they were willing to face the fiery furnace rather than compromise their faith. Kidmin teaches families the importance of standing firm in their beliefs, even when faced with adversity or pressures to conform.

Kidmin also empowers families to engage in intentional conversations about faith and worldview. Parents and guardians are equipped with resources and tools to discuss challenging topics and address the secular influences their children encounter. These conversations strengthen family bonds, build a solid foundation of faith, and equip children to make wise choices based on biblical principles.

As families anchor themselves in the truth of God's Word, they become powerful witnesses to the world around them. Just as Shadrach, Meshach, and Abednego's faith stood out in a culture that demanded conformity, families rooted in God's truth can shine as beacons of hope and light in their communities. Their unwavering commitment to God's principles becomes a testimony to the transformative power of the gospel.

Heavenly Father, we thank You for the gift of Kidmin in the lives of families. Help us to anchor ourselves in the truth of Your Word amidst the secular influences of church and culture. Give us the strength to stand firm in our faith, just as Shadrach, Meshach, and Abednego did. Equip us to navigate the challenges and pressures that our families face, and empower us to pass on a legacy of faith to the next generation. In Jesus' name, we pray. Amen.

Takeaway

Kidmin matters greatly to the family because it equips them with the truth of the Scriptures and strengthens their faith amidst secular influences. Like Shadrach, Meshach, and Abednego, families are called to stand firm in their beliefs and refuse to compromise their devotion to God. By anchoring themselves in the unchanging truths of God's Word, families become powerful witnesses in a world that demands conformity. Let us embrace the role of Kidmin in equipping families with biblical truths, nurturing community, and empowering them to navigate the challenges of church and culture with unwavering faith. IT MATTERS.

_____

_____

_____

_____

_____

_____

_____

_____

IN CHILDREN'S MINISTRY,
WE HAVE THE PRIVILEGE OF
TEACHING THE

next generation

TO LOVE JESUS.

WEEK 19 : IT MATTERS TO THE FAMILY
The Power of Church–Parent Partnership in Kidmin

"These commandments that I give you today are to be on your hearts. Impress them on your children. Talk about them when you sit at home and when you walk along the road, when you lie down and when you get up."
Deuteronomy 6:6-7

Kidmin matters greatly to the family because of the power of the church-parent partnership. When the church and family work together, a powerful synergy is created, leading to effective discipleship and spiritual growth in children.

The church-parent partnership in Kidmin is a powerful force for nurturing the faith of children. When the church and parents work together as a team, they create a supportive and dynamic environment for children to grow spiritually. This partnership recognizes that the home and the church are both essential in shaping a child's faith and character.

The church plays a crucial role in providing resources, teaching, and a community of believers who walk alongside children in their faith journey. Through Kidmin programs, children are equipped with biblical knowledge, encouraged to engage in worship, and given opportunities to serve others. The church creates a spiritual foundation upon which parents can build, providing a solid framework for faith development.

On the other hand, parents are called to be the primary spiritual leaders in their children's lives. They have the unique privilege and responsibility of imparting biblical truths and modeling a vibrant faith. The partnership with the church empowers parents, providing them with resources, support, and a network of like-minded believers who can offer guidance and encouragement along the way.

Deuteronomy 6:6-7 instructs parents to impress God's commandments on their children and to engage in intentional conversations about faith throughout daily life. This passage emphasizes the importance of holistic discipleship, where spiritual formation is not limited to a specific time or place but is woven into the fabric of everyday experiences.

When the church and parents work together, spiritual lessons are reinforced and internalized in the hearts and minds of children. The church provides the teaching and resources, while parents play a vital role in cultivating an environment where faith is nurtured and lived out. This partnership ensures that children receive consistent and comprehensive spiritual guidance that extends beyond the walls of the church.

The church-parent partnership also fosters a sense of community and accountability. It brings parents together, creating opportunities for sharing experiences, learning from one another, and praying for each other's children. As parents witness the spiritual growth of their own children and others within the church, they are inspired and encouraged in their own parenting journey.

Moreover, this partnership models a holistic approach to discipleship for children. When they see their parents actively engaged in their faith, seeking God's guidance, and participating in church activities, children learn the importance of a vibrant and authentic relationship with God. They witness firsthand how faith is integrated into every aspect of life, empowering them to do the same.

As we reflect on the power of the church-parent partnership in Kidmin, let us recognize the importance of teamwork and collaboration. Let us celebrate the unique roles of the church and parents in shaping the spiritual lives of children.

Heavenly Father, we thank You for the gift of the church-parent partnership in Kidmin. Help us to work together as a team, recognizing the vital roles each plays in shaping the faith of children. Strengthen our collaboration and empower us to create an environment where children can grow spiritually. May our partnership reflect Your love and grace, inspiring children to follow You wholeheartedly. In Jesus' name, we pray. Amen.

Takeaway

The church-parent partnership in Kidmin is a powerful force for nurturing the faith of children. When the church and parents work together as a team, effective discipleship happens. The church provides resources, teaching, and community, while parents serve as the primary spiritual leaders in their children's lives. This partnership reinforces spiritual lessons, models holistic discipleship, and fosters a sense of community. Let us embrace the power of the church-parent partnership, recognizing its significance in shaping the next generation's faith. IT MATTERS.

_____

_____

_____

_____

_____

_____

_____

_____

CHILDREN'S MINISTRY IS WHERE
Tiny hands
RECEIVE GOD'S
GREAT PROMISES.

WEEK 20 : IT MATTERS TO THE FAMILY
Family Faith Builders: Empowering Parents through Kidmin

"So Christ himself gave the apostles, the prophets, the evangelists, the pastors and teachers, to equip his people for works of service, so that the body of Christ may be built up until we all reach unity in the faith and in the knowledge of the Son of God and become mature, attaining to the whole measure of the fullness of Christ."
Ephesians 4:11-13

Kidmin matters greatly to families because it empowers parents to be the primary spiritual influencers in their children's lives. The role of a children's pastor is not to replace parents but to equip and support them in their God-given responsibility.

Parents hold a unique position as the primary spiritual influencers in their children's lives. God has entrusted parents with the responsibility of imparting faith, teaching biblical truths, and modeling a vibrant relationship with Him. Kidmin recognizes and supports this vital role, serving to empower parents to fulfill their God-given calling.

In Ephesians 4:11-13, we see that Christ has given apostles, prophets, evangelists, pastors, and teachers to equip His people for works of service. The primary goal is not for these ministry leaders to do all the work themselves but to equip the body of Christ for ministry. This includes parents, who play a crucial role in the spiritual development of their children.

Kidmin, with its dedicated children's pastors and teachers, serves as a valuable resource for parents. It provides tools, curriculum, and guidance to assist parents in teaching biblical truths effectively. The role of the children's pastor is not to replace parents but to come alongside them, equipping and supporting them in their journey of raising godly children.

Through Kidmin, parents gain a deeper understanding of how to integrate faith into everyday life. They learn practical ways to engage their children in spiritual conversations, create teachable moments, and apply biblical principles to real-life situations. Kidmin offers resources that enable parents to walk alongside their children as they navigate challenges and grow in their faith.

The partnership between Kidmin and parents also helps foster a sense of unity within the family. As parents engage with the spiritual teachings and experiences provided by Kidmin, they become more equipped to guide their children on their faith journey. This unity strengthens family bonds, creating an environment where children witness their parents' genuine commitment to God and His Word.

Furthermore, Kidmin empowers parents to model a vibrant relationship with God. Children observe their parents' attitudes, values, and behaviors, and they learn from their examples. When parents actively engage in their own spiritual growth, seeking God's guidance and demonstrating a genuine love for Him, children are inspired to do the same.

In this partnership, children's pastors and teachers have the privilege of equipping parents with knowledge, tools, and encouragement. They help parents recognize their unique role and the impact they have on their children's spiritual lives. The children's pastor's primary job is not to replace parents but to empower them to be the primary spiritual influencers in their children's lives.

As parents embrace their role as spiritual leaders, they play a vital part in building up the body of Christ. When families are grounded in faith, walking in unity, and growing in their knowledge of God, the entire church is strengthened. The body of Christ becomes a powerful force for spreading the gospel and making disciples.

Heavenly Father, we thank You for the gift of parenting and the responsibility to be primary spiritual influencers in our children's lives. We recognize the important role that Kidmin plays in empowering parents. Help us to embrace this partnership, seeking wisdom and guidance as we raise our children in the ways of the Lord. Equip us to model a vibrant relationship with You, leading our children by example. In Jesus' name, we pray. Amen.

Takeaway

Kidmin matters greatly to families because it empowers parents as the primary spiritual influencers in their children's lives. The role of children's pastors is to equip and support parents in their God-given responsibility. Kidmin provides resources, guidance, and a partnership that helps parents navigate their roles effectively. As parents embrace their calling, they play a crucial part in building up the body of Christ. Let us recognize and celebrate the partnership between Kidmin and parents, knowing that when parents are empowered, the entire family and church community thrive. IT MATTERS.

_____

_____

_____

_____

_____

_____

_____

_____

KIDS ARE NOT JUST
SPECTATORS;
THEY ARE
ACTIVE PARTICIPANTS IN
God's kingdom.

WEEK 21 : IT MATTERS TO THE FAMILY
Real Talk, Real Solutions: How Kidmin Helps Families Address Life's Challenges

"For the word of God is alive and active. Sharper than any double-edged sword, it penetrates even to dividing soul and spirit, joints and marrow; it judges the thoughts and attitudes of the heart."
Hebrews 4:12

Kidmin matters greatly to the family because it provides essential help in addressing the real-life challenges they face. In today's culture, families are bombarded with pressures and attacks that can leave them feeling overwhelmed and disconnected. However, as Kidmin leaders, we have the privilege and responsibility to come alongside families, helping them navigate these challenges by grounding them in the truths and promises of Scripture.

In today's world, families encounter numerous challenges that can shake the very foundations of their lives. The culture bombards them with conflicting messages, distorted values, and unattainable expectations. Moreover, the family unit itself is under attack like never before. The enemy seeks to divide, discourage, and dismantle the bonds of love and unity within families. In the face of these challenges, Kidmin plays a vital role in providing families with the support, guidance, and grounding they need.

Hebrews 4:12 describes the power of God's Word as alive and active. It cuts through the noise and confusion of the world, penetrating deep into the core of our being. The Word of God, like a double-edged sword, discerns and exposes the thoughts and attitudes of our hearts. It provides the necessary clarity, truth, and wisdom to address the real-life challenges that families face.

As Kidmin leaders, we have the privilege of sharing the truths and promises of Scripture with families. We have the opportunity to teach and guide parents and children in understanding and applying God's Word to their everyday lives. By doing so, we help families build a solid foundation rooted in God's truth, equipping them to face the challenges of the world with confidence and resilience.

In Kidmin, we come alongside families to address the cultural pressures they encounter. We create a safe space where families can openly discuss and navigate these challenges together. Through age-appropriate lessons, discussions, and activities, we address real-life topics that families grapple with, offering biblical insights and perspectives that bring clarity and hope.

Moreover, Kidmin provides families with practical tools to apply God's Word in their daily lives. We offer resources that help parents and children develop spiritual disciplines, cultivate healthy relationships, and make godly choices. By equipping families with these tools, we empower them to live out their faith authentically and navigate the challenges they face with wisdom and discernment.

Kidmin also fosters a sense of community among families. It provides a network of support where families can find encouragement, prayer, and fellowship. Within this community, families can share their struggles, celebrate their victories, and grow together in their faith. The mutual support and accountability offered by Kidmin help families stay connected and strong in their journey.

Ultimately, Kidmin points families to the unchanging truths and promises of Scripture. In a world that constantly shifts and changes, the Word of God remains a firm foundation. It provides families with a timeless and reliable guide that leads them through life's challenges. Through the power of God's Word, families discover hope, healing, restoration, and transformation.

As Kidmin leaders, we have the sacred task of helping families know and be grounded in the truths and promises of Scripture. We have the privilege of pointing them to the One who can bring peace, strength, and victory in the midst of their challenges. By cultivating love and reverence for God's Word within families, we empower them to navigate life's complexities with wisdom, faith, and resilience.

Heavenly Father, we thank You for the gift of Kidmin and the opportunity to come alongside families in their journey. Help us to address the real-life challenges they face, guiding them with the power and relevance of Your Word. Strengthen us to provide the support, resources, and wisdom families need to navigate these challenges. May Your Word bring healing, restoration, and trans-formation to every family. In Jesus' name, we pray. Amen.

Takeaway

Kidmin matters greatly to the family because it addresses their real-life challenges. By grounding families in the truths and promises of Scripture, Kidmin empowers them to navigate the pressures and attacks of culture. As Kidmin leaders, we have the privilege and responsibility to provide support, guidance, and resources that help families address these challenges. Let us remain steadfast in our commitment to help families know and be grounded in the unchanging truths and promises of God's Word. IT MATTERS.

_____

_____

_____

_____

_____

_____

_____

_____

IN CHILDREN'S MINISTRY,
WE BUILD A
foundation of faith
THAT CAN WITHSTAND
ANY STORM.

WEEK 22 : IT MATTERS TO THE FAMILY
Legacy Builders: Kidmin's Impact on Grandparent–Grandchild Relationships

"So that you, your children and their children after them may fear the Lord your God as long as you live by keeping all his decrees and commands that I give you, and so that you may enjoy long life."
Deuteronomy 6:2

Kidmin leaders, we understand the profound impact that grandparents have in the lives of their grandchildren. As we strive to build a strong foundation of faith in the younger generation, we must recognize the crucial role that grandparents play. In Deuteronomy 6:2, we see the significance of passing down God's decrees and commands to future generations.

The commandments laid out in Deuteronomy 6:2 remind us that our role as Kidmin leaders extends beyond the children we directly minister to. We have the privilege of partnering with grandparents, recognizing their wisdom and influence in the lives of their grandchildren. As children's pastors, we must equip and support grandparents as they pass down their faith to the next generation.

In children's ministry, we acknowledge that grandparents bring a unique perspective and experience that enriches the faith-building process. They have witnessed God's faithfulness throughout their lives, and their testimonies can profoundly impact their grandchildren's spiritual development. It is our responsibility to create an environment where grandparents feel empowered and equipped to pass down the truths and values of Scripture.

We provide resources, training, and support to help grandparents navigate their vital role as spiritual influencers. Through age-appropriate curriculum, activities, and discussions, we assist grandparents in engaging their grandchildren in meaningful conversations about faith. By offering practical tools and strategies, we enable grandparents to share their wisdom, life lessons, and love for God with their grandchildren.

Additionally, we foster intergenerational connections within our Kidmin community, creating opportunities for grandparents to connect with other families and share their experiences. We facilitate events and gatherings that encourage these connections, recognizing the strength and support that comes from intergenerational relationships. Through these interactions, grandparents can impart their faith and provide a sense of belonging and spiritual heritage to their grandchildren.

We understand that the challenges faced by today's families are different from those of previous generations. In this rapidly changing world, grandparents often find themselves navigating complex cultural influences alongside their grandchildren. In Kidmin, we address these challenges and equip grandparents with biblical insights and practical guidance to help them guide their grandchildren in making godly choices.

Furthermore, we encourage grandparents to cover their grandchildren in prayer. Prayer is a powerful tool that grandparents can utilize to intercede on behalf of their grandchildren's spiritual well-being. We remind grandparents of the importance of regularly lifting up their grandchildren in prayer, trusting in God's faithfulness to work in their lives.

Kidmin leaders, let us recognize the vital role that grandparents play in raising mighty kingdom builders. As we partner with them, we come alongside them to offer resources, support, and encouragement. By equipping grandparents, we empower them to leave a lasting legacy of faith for generations to come. Together, we can build a community where the influence of grandparents is valued and celebrated.

Heavenly Father, we thank You for the significant role that grandparents play in raising mighty kingdom builders. We pray for Kidmin leaders as we partner with grandparents to pass down faith to future generations. Equip us to provide the necessary resources, support, and guidance to empower grandparents in their spiritual influence. May we build a strong community where the wisdom and experience of grandparents are cherished and celebrated. In Jesus' name, we pray. Amen.

Takeaway

Kidmin leaders, grandparents have a profound impact on the lives of their grandchildren. As we strive to build a strong foundation of faith, we must recognize and support their essential role. By equipping and empowering grandparents, we enable them to pass down their faith, wisdom, and love for God to their grandchildren. Let us foster intergenerational connections, provide resources, and offer support to grandparents as they raise mighty kingdom builders. Together, we can leave a lasting legacy of faith that will impact future generations. IT MATTERS.

CHILDREN'S MINISTRY IS NOT
A JOB; IT'S A

joyful calling

TO INVEST IN ETERNITY.

WEEK 23 : IT MATTERS TO THE FAMILY
Strength in Numbers: Kidmin's Impact on Single Parents

"Carry each other's burdens, and in this way you will fulfill the law of Christ."
Galatians 6:2

Kidmin matters significantly because it extends valuable help, support, and connection to single parents. In today's world, the number of single parents navigating the journey of parenthood alone is increasing. Being a parent is challenging, and when faced with the unique set of trials that come with being a single parent, the need for support becomes even more crucial. As kidmin leaders, we have the privilege and responsibility to come alongside these single parents, offering them the love, care, and resources they need.

Today, more than ever, single parents are shouldering the weight of parenthood alone. Statistics show a significant rise in the number of single-parent households, highlighting the need for support and community. As kidmin leaders, we recognize the challenges and struggles that single parents face and the importance of providing a safe and nurturing environment where they can find help and connection.

Galatians 6:2 reminds us of our responsibility to carry each other's burdens. We are called to walk alongside one another, offering support and assistance in times of need. This biblical principle holds special significance for single parents, who often face unique challenges, such as balancing work and parenting responsibilities, financial strains, and feelings of loneliness or isolation. Kidmin can play a vital role in addressing these needs and providing a sense of community and support.

As kidmin leaders, we have the opportunity to offer valuable help and resources to single parents. We can provide practical support by offering childcare during services or special events, giving single parents an opportunity to participate fully and connect with others. Additionally, we can organize parenting workshops or seminars that address topics specific to single parenting, offering guidance and strategies to navigate the unique challenges they face.

Moreover, Kidmin can serve as a safe space where single parents can find encouragement, acceptance, and understanding. By creating an atmosphere of love and support, we can offer single parents a place to share their joys, concerns, and struggles without judgment. Through intentional relationships and small group gatherings, we foster connections that help single parents realize they are not alone on this journey.

Kidmin can also provide spiritual support to single parents. We recognize that spiritual growth and nourishment are essential aspects of their lives. By offering relevant and relatable teachings, resources, and opportunities for prayer and worship, we can help single parents deepen their faith and find solace and strength in their relationship with God. Kidmin can equip them to lean on their faith as they navigate the challenges of parenting alone.

In addition, Kidmin leaders can connect single parents with other supportive resources within the church community. This may include connecting them with mentors or support groups specifically designed for single parents. By establishing partnerships with local organizations, we can expand the support network available to single parents, ensuring they have access to valuable services and assistance.

Through our actions, words, and genuine care, we demonstrate the love of Christ to single parents. By extending a helping hand, being a listening ear, and offering practical and emotional support, we fulfill the call to carry one another's burdens. Kidmin becomes a beacon of hope and encouragement, reminding single parents that they are valued, cherished, and supported within the church community.

Heavenly Father, we thank You for the gift of Kidmin and the opportunity to support single parents on their journey of parenthood. We lift up single parents to You, asking for Your guidance, strength, and provision. May Kidmin serve as a place of comfort, support, and connection, offering practical help and spiritual nourishment. Help us, as kidmin leaders, to extend Your love and care to single parents, fulfilling the call to carry one another's burdens. In Jesus' name, we pray. Amen.

Takeaway

Kidmin matters greatly to single parents, as it provides the help, support, and connection they need on their journey of parenthood. By extending practical assistance, creating a sense of community, and offering spiritual support, Kidmin becomes a lifeline for single parents. As kidmin leaders, let us be intentional in providing resources, fostering connections, and demonstrating the love of Christ to single parents, fulfilling the call to carry one another's burdens. Together, we can create a supportive environment where single parents find strength, encouragement, and the assurance that they are not alone on their parenting journey. IT MATTERS.

_____

_____

_____

_____

_____

_____

_____

_____

KIDS ARE NOT JUST THE FUTURE;
THEY ARE CARRIERS OF

God's presence

TODAY.

WEEK 24 : IT MATTERS TO THE FAMILY
A Place of Belonging: Kidmin's Inclusive Community for Special Needs Families

"Be devoted to one another in love. Honor one another above yourselves."
Romans 12:10

Kidmin matters immensely because it extends love and support to families impacted by special needs. Within our communities, there is a significant population of parents caring for children with disabilities. These parents face unique challenges and are in great need of love, understanding, and support from their church family. As Kidmin leaders, we have a remarkable opportunity to create connection points and foster relationships that can bring immense joy and support to these families.

Within our church families, there are parents who courageously navigate the complexities of caring for children with special needs. They often face unique challenges that can be physically, emotionally, and spiritually demanding. As Kidmin leaders, we recognize the critical importance of extending love, understanding, and support to these families, who may often feel overlooked.

In Romans 12:10, we are called to be devoted to one another in love and to honor one another above ourselves. This biblical principle speaks directly to the heart of Kidmin's role in supporting families impacted by special needs. We are called to cultivate a culture of love, acceptance, and inclusivity where these families can find a place of belonging and support.

One of the key ways Kidmin can make a significant impact is by creating a welcoming and inclusive environment for children with special needs. This may involve making adaptations or modifications to the curriculum, physical spaces, and activities to ensure accessibility and accommodate individual needs. By doing so, we communicate to these families that their presence is valued and that we are committed to journeying alongside them.

In addition to providing inclusive spaces, Kidmin can foster genuine relationships with families impacted by special needs. By taking the time to listen, understand, and empathize with their unique experiences, we demonstrate our commitment to walking alongside them. We can offer practical support, such as respite care, or provide resources and information that can assist them in navigating the challenges they face.

Kidmin also has the opportunity to create connection points for families impacted by special needs to build relationships with other families and church members. By organizing events, support groups, or special programs, we create spaces where families can connect, share their joys and struggles, and support one another. These connections can become a source of tremendous strength, encouragement, and joy for families navigating the journey of special needs.

Furthermore, it is essential for Kidmin leaders to educate and equip themselves and their teams on how to effectively engage and support children with special needs. Training on inclusive practices, communication strategies, and understanding specific disabilities can make a significant difference in meeting the needs of these families. By fostering a culture of learning and growth, we ensure that our ministry is continuously improving and better-serving families impacted by special needs.

Above all, Kidmin must be a place where families impacted by special needs experience the love of Christ in tangible ways. We are called to demonstrate unconditional love, grace, and acceptance to these families, just as Christ has done for us. Our aim is to create a safe and nurturing environment where families feel seen, valued, and supported, fostering an atmosphere of hope, joy, and belonging.

Heavenly Father, we thank You for the families impacted by special needs within our church community. We lift them up to You, asking for Your love, strength, and provision. Help us, as Kidmin leaders, to extend Your love and support to these families, creating a welcoming and inclusive environment where they can thrive. Guide us in fostering relationships, providing practical help, and equipping our teams to serve them better. May Your love shine through us as we honor and support these families. In Jesus' name, we pray. Amen.

Takeaway

Kidmin matters greatly to families impacted by special needs. By creating a welcoming, inclusive, and supportive environment, we demonstrate Christ's love to these families. Through adaptation, genuine relationships, connection points, and education, we extend practical and emotional support. Let us honor and support these families, journeying alongside them with love and understanding. In doing so, we reflect the love of Christ and create a space where families impacted by special needs can experience the joy, acceptance, and support they desperately need. IT MATTERS.

_____

_____

_____

_____

_____

_____

_____

_____

IN CHILDREN'S MINISTRY,
WE ARE WATERING THE
seeds of faith,
TRUSTING GOD
FOR THE HARVEST.

WEEK 25 : IT MATTERS TO THE FAMILY
Restoring Family Time: Kidmin's Influence on Busy Lives

"Children are a heritage from the Lord, offspring a reward from him."
Psalm 127:3

Kidmin matters significantly because it offers a beacon of truth and support to today's busy families. In a world where families are bombarded with messages about the need for endless extracurricular activities and societal pressures, we, as Kidmin leaders, have the opportunity to provide a space where the truth of Scripture can be heard. By offering a balanced perspective on successful parenting and the value of quality time, we can help alleviate the noise and bring peace and clarity to busy families.

In the hustle and bustle of today's society, families find themselves constantly bombarded with messages about what it takes to be successful. The pressure to participate in endless extracurricular activities and maintain a packed schedule can leave parents and children feeling overwhelmed and stretched thin. As Kidmin leaders, we have the unique opportunity to offer a counter-narrative based on the truth of Scripture and God's design for family life.

Psalm 127:3 reminds us that children are a heritage from the Lord, a precious reward. In a culture that often equates success with busyness and external achievements, this verse reminds us of the true value and significance of our children and family life. It encourages us to prioritize the well-being and spiritual growth of our children above all else.

As Kidmin leaders, we can partner with parents to help them navigate the pressures of today's busy world. We have the privilege of sharing the truth of Scripture, teaching parents and children that success is not solely defined by achievements or a packed schedule but by nurturing and investing in their relationship with God and one another.

Through Kidmin, we can offer a balanced perspective on parenting, emphasizing the importance of quality time and intentional moments of connection. We can provide resources and practical tools to help families create space for meaningful conversations, prayer, and reflection. By focusing on these vital aspects, we help families cultivate a foundation of faith, love, and connection that will have a lasting impact.

Additionally, Kidmin can serve as a respite for busy families, providing a place of refuge and rejuvenation. Through engaging and age-appropriate programs, we offer children a safe and nurturing environment where they can experience the joy of authentic worship, biblical teachings, and meaningful relationships. By partnering with parents, we become a source of support, encouragement, and guidance, offering them reassurance that they are not alone in their journey.

Moreover, Kidmin can foster a community where families can find support and connection with like-minded individuals. We can organize family events, parent gatherings, and small groups that create opportunities for fellowship, encouragement, and shared experiences. By providing spaces for families to connect and build relationships, we alleviate the sense of isolation that can often accompany a busy lifestyle.

In our efforts to support today's busy families, it is vital that we continuously point them back to the truth of God's Word. We remind them that success is not found in busyness and external achievements but in faithfulness to God's calling as parents. We encourage them to find rest and strength in Him, trusting in His provision and guidance.

Heavenly Father, we thank You for the families in our midst, navigating the challenges of a busy world. We lift them up to You, asking for Your wisdom and guidance. Help us, as Kidmin leaders, to provide support and truth to busy families, nurturing their faith and offering respite from the pressures of the world. May our ministry be a source of peace, clarity, and connection, pointing families back to Your design for family life. In Jesus' name, we pray. Amen.

Takeaway

Kidmin matters greatly to today's busy families as we offer a counter-narrative to the pressures of society. By sharing the truth of Scripture and prioritizing quality time, we help families find peace and clarity amidst the noise. Through engaging programs, support, and a nurturing community, we create spaces where families can grow in their faith, foster meaningful connections, and experience the joy of being present with one another. Let us continue to guide and support today's busy families, reminding them of the true value and significance of their journey together. IT MATTERS.

CHILDREN'S MINISTRY
IS WHERE

young voices

LEARN TO PRAISE
THE CREATOR.

WEEK 26 : IT MATTERS TO THE FAMILY
Beyond the Church Walls: Kidmin's Role in Equipping Families on Mission

"In the same way, let your light shine before others, that they may see your good deeds and glorify your Father in heaven."
Matthew 5:16

Kidmin matters immensely because it plays a vital role in equipping missional families. In today's world, many people are not stepping through the doors of the church. It is crucial, now more than ever, for our church families to be empowered and equipped to live out their faith and be on a mission throughout their daily lives. As Kidmin leaders, we have the important responsibility to empower our children and parents to be the light of Christ in their communities.

In our current cultural climate, many people are not actively seeking out a church community. The mission field is no longer confined to a specific building or gathering. As Kidmin leaders, we recognize the need to equip our church families to live out their faith in their everyday lives, engaging with others in a way that reflects the love and truth of Jesus Christ.

Matthew 5:16 reminds us of the importance of letting our light shine before others. Our mission is to equip and empower families to be a light in their communities, workplaces, schools, and social circles. By intentionally living out their faith and demonstrating God's love through their actions and words, they have the opportunity to draw others to the message and hope of Jesus.

Kidmin plays a crucial role in equipping families to be missional. We provide a foundation of biblical teaching, instilling in children and parents the knowledge and understanding of God's Word. We teach them about the love and grace of Jesus, as well as the significance of sharing that love with others. By empowering families with a deep understanding of the Gospel, we equip them to engage in meaningful conversations and to live out their faith authentically.

Additionally, Kidmin provides practical tools and resources to support families in their missional endeavors. We can teach children and parents how to engage in intentional acts of kindness, service, and outreach. We can encourage families to pray for their communities and to seek opportunities to meet the needs of those around them. By providing guidance and support, we help families navigate the challenges and joys of being on a mission.

Furthermore, Kidmin fosters a sense of community and accountability within families. We create spaces where families can connect with other like-minded individuals, share experiences, and encourage one another in their missional efforts. By fostering these relationships, we provide a support system that helps families stay focused and inspired in their mission.

In our efforts to equip missional families, it is essential to highlight the value of both parents and children in this calling. We recognize that children have a unique ability to influence their peers and share the love of Jesus with their friends and classmates. Kidmin can empower children to live as lights in their schools, sports teams, and neighborhoods. Simultaneously, we encourage parents to lead by example, demonstrating a Christ-like attitude and lifestyle in their workplaces, social circles, and everyday interactions.

As Kidmin leaders, we must continually inspire and challenge families to live out their faith beyond the walls of the church. We can provide ongoing support, training, and resources that empower families to make a difference in their communities. By encouraging them to see their everyday lives as a mission field, we help them understand that they have the power to impact and transform the lives of those around them.

Heavenly Father, we thank You for the privilege of equipping missional families through Kidmin. We pray for the families in our care, asking for Your guidance and empowerment. Help us to instill in them a passion for living out their faith and being a light in their communities. Equip them with the knowledge, tools, and courage they need to be effective ambassadors for Christ. May their lives attract others to the message and hope of Jesus. In His name, we pray. Amen.

Takeaway

Kidmin matters greatly in equipping missional families to live out their faith beyond the walls of the church. By providing a strong foundation in God's Word, practical tools and resources, and a supportive community, we empower families to be the light of Christ in their communities. Let us continue to inspire and challenge families to see their everyday lives as a mission field, recognizing their significant role in drawing others to the message and hope of Jesus. Together, we can make a lasting impact in the lives of those around us. IT MATTERS.

KIDS ARE NOT JUST
LITTLE PEOPLE;
THEY ARE GIFTS WITH
unique purposes.

WEEK 27 : IT MATTERS TO KIDS
The Gospel is for Kids Now

"And he said: 'Truly I tell you, unless you change and become like little children, you will never enter the kingdom of heaven. Therefore, whoever takes the lowly position of this child is the greatest in the kingdom of heaven.'"
Matthew 18:3-4

Kidmin matters deeply because it recognizes that the gospel is for kids now. Jesus Himself emphasized the importance of childlike faith and declared that unless we become like little children, we cannot enter the kingdom of heaven. As Kidmin leaders, we have the privilege and responsibility to nurture the childlike faith in children, guiding them in their journey of following Jesus.

The words of Jesus in Matthew 18:3-4 hold profound significance for our understanding of Kidmin's role in sharing the gospel with children. Jesus said, "Truly I tell you, unless you change and become like little children, you will never enter the kingdom of heaven. Therefore, whoever takes the lowly position of this child is the greatest in the kingdom of heaven."

These words remind us that childlike faith is not only welcomed but essential in our journey with Jesus. Children possess a natural openness, trust, and dependence that are foundational to a vibrant relationship with God. Kidmin leaders have the incredible opportunity to foster and nurture this childlike faith, guiding children as they develop a deep and personal connection with Jesus.

What we do in Kidmin is far more than providing childcare or entertainment. We are entrusted with the task of sharing the life-transforming truth of the gospel and helping children cultivate a genuine and vibrant faith. By teaching them about Jesus' love, sacrifice, and the hope found in Him, we create an environment where children can encounter His presence and experience His grace.

Jesus' words remind us that childlike faith involves humility, trust, and a willingness to receive and believe the truths of the gospel. Children are naturally inclined to trust and depend on others, and their hearts are receptive to God's Word. As Kidmin leaders, we have the responsibility to help children understand the gospel message in a way that resonates with their hearts and empowers them to follow Jesus wholeheartedly.

Furthermore, children have the unique ability to exemplify qualities that Jesus values in His kingdom. They often display humility, teachability, and a readiness to embrace the lowly position of a child. By encouraging children to live out these qualities, we create a culture of humility and service that reflects the heart of Jesus.

Kidmin plays a significant role in fostering childlike faith and encouraging children to embrace the lowly position of a child. Through engaging Bible lessons, worship, and discipleship, we create spaces where children can encounter God's truth and experience His love. By providing a supportive community and mentors who model Christ-like humility and servanthood, we inspire children to grow in their faith and become influential kingdom builders.

The impact of sharing the gospel with children at a young age is immeasurable. When children embrace Jesus with childlike faith, their lives are transformed, and they become powerful agents of God's kingdom. As Kidmin leaders, we have the honor of nurturing this faith and guiding children in their spiritual journey, equipping them to impact their families, schools, and communities for Jesus.

Heavenly Father, we thank You for the privilege of sharing the gospel with children through Kidmin. We pray for the children in our care, asking for Your Holy Spirit to work in their hearts and draw them to Jesus. Give us wisdom, patience, and creativity as we teach and mentor them. May they embrace childlike faith, humbly following Jesus and growing in their love for You. In Jesus' name, we pray. Amen.

Takeaway

Kidmin matters deeply because the gospel is for kids now. As Kidmin leaders, we have the incredible privilege and responsibility to nurture child-like faith in children, guiding them in their journey of following Jesus. Let us embrace the qualities of humility, trust, and teachability that children exemplify, allowing their childlike faith to inspire and challenge us in our own walk with God. May we encourage children to embrace the lowly position of a child and grow in their love for Jesus, becoming influential kingdom builders in their families, schools, and communities. IT MATTERS.

_____

_____

_____

_____

_____

_____

_____

_____

IN CHILDREN'S MINISTRY,
WE ARE SHAPING
world-changers
FOR GOD'S KINGDOM.

WEEK 28 : IT MATTERS TO KIDS
From Little Seeds to Mighty Oaks: Why Kidmin Matters in Spiritual Formation

"For the grace of God has appeared that offers salvation to all people. It teaches us to say 'No' to ungodliness and worldly passions, and to live self-controlled, upright, and godly lives in this present age, while we wait for the blessed hope—the appearing of the glory of our great God and Savior, Jesus Christ, who gave himself for us to redeem us from all wickedness and to purify for himself a people that are his very own, eager to do what is good."
Titus 2:11-14

Kidmin matters deeply because it recognizes the potential for children to become grounded in their faith. Spiritual formation can begin at an early age, and what we do in children's ministry has a direct and lasting impact on their journey of faith.

The words of Titus 2:11-14 highlight the transformative power of God's grace and its role in shaping our lives as believers. Kidmin provides a nurturing environment where children can encounter God's grace and learn to live according to His teachings. We have the opportunity to introduce children to the message of salvation and guide them in developing a vibrant and personal relationship with Jesus Christ. By teaching them to say "No" to ungodliness and embrace a godly lifestyle, we empower them to live self-controlled and upright lives, even at a young age.

What we do in Kidmin goes beyond mere teaching or providing activities. We are called to equip children with the knowledge of God's Word and help them apply biblical principles in their daily lives. By presenting the truth of God's grace and His redemptive work through Jesus Christ, we instill in children a deep understanding of their need for salvation and the transformative power of a personal relationship with Jesus.

Kidmin offers a safe and supportive community where children can ask questions, seek guidance, and explore their faith. Through engaging Bible lessons, worship, and discipleship, we create an environment that fosters spiritual growth and nurtures a sense of belonging. As Kidmin leaders, we have the privilege of walking alongside children, mentoring them, and encouraging their pursuit of a godly life.

The impact of Kidmin on children's spiritual formation is significant. When children are grounded in their faith at an early age, they are equipped to navigate the challenges and temptations of this present age. They learn to discern right from wrong, resist worldly passions, and pursue a life that honors God. As they grow in their understanding of God's grace and the hope found in Jesus Christ, they become eager to do what is good and make a positive impact in their spheres of influence.

By helping children develop a firm foundation in their faith, Kidmin empowers them to live out their identity as God's own people. It prepares them to face the world with confidence, integrity, and a passion for doing what is pleasing to God. The investment we make in children's spiritual formation through Kidmin has the potential to shape their entire lives and contribute to the advancement of God's kingdom.

Heavenly Father, we thank You for the privilege of serving in Kidmin and having the opportunity to impact children's lives for eternity. We pray for the children in our care, asking for Your Holy Spirit to work in their hearts and guide them in their journey of faith. Grant us wisdom, patience, and creativity as we teach and mentor them. May they be grounded in Your grace, living self-controlled, upright, and godly lives that bring honor to Your name. In Jesus' name, we pray. Amen.

Takeaway

Kidmin matters deeply because it provides a space where children can become grounded in their faith. By teaching them about God's grace, salvation, and the transformative power of a relationship with Jesus Christ, we equip them to live self-controlled, upright, and godly lives. Through the nurturing environment of Kidmin, children are empowered to say "No" to ungodliness and embrace a lifestyle that honors God. Let us invest in children's spiritual formation, knowing that what we do in Kidmin has a lasting impact on their journey of faith and their ability to navigate the challenges of this present age. IT MATTERS.

_____

_____

_____

_____

_____

_____

_____

_____

CHILDREN'S MINISTRY
IS NOT A STEPPING STONE;
IT'S A
legacy of faith.

WEEK 29 : IT MATTERS TO KIDS
Better Together: Why Kidmin Matters in Cultivating Meaningful Connections

"As iron sharpens iron, so one person sharpens another."
Proverbs 27:17

Kidmin matters deeply because it recognizes the importance of community and friendship in the lives of children. Children's ministry creates an environment where kids can connect with their peers, cultivate meaningful friendships, and experience a sense of belonging within a supportive Christian community.

The verse in Proverbs 27:17 beautifully illustrates the impact of community and friendship in our lives. Just as iron blades are sharpened through friction and interaction, our lives are enriched and strengthened when we engage in relationships with others.

Children's ministry provides a unique space where children can form connections and build friendships. Within the vibrant and nurturing environment of children's ministry, kids have the opportunity to meet and interact with their peers who share a common faith. Through engaging activities, group discussions, and collaborative learning experiences, children can develop meaningful connections that can last a lifetime.

In the context of Kidmin, friendship extends beyond mere companionship. It becomes a foundation for discipleship and spiritual growth. As children engage with one another, they have the chance to encourage, support, and sharpen each other's faith. They learn from one another, ask questions together, and experience the beauty of the Christian community.

Kidmin also provides an avenue for kids to connect with adults and leaders who can pour into their lives. As children interact with caring and supportive mentors, they have access to wisdom, guidance, and role models who can help them navigate life's challenges and inspire them in their walk with God. These relationships foster a sense of belonging and create opportunities for genuine discipleship to occur.

Within the community of Kidmin, children experience a safe and accepting space where they can be themselves. They find encouragement to express their thoughts, share their struggles, and celebrate their victories. Through this shared journey, they learn important values such as empathy, kindness, and forgiveness. They witness the beauty of diverse perspectives and discover the richness of unity in Christ.

As Kidmin leaders, our role goes beyond providing programs and activities. We have the privilege of creating an environment that nurtures genuine connections and friendships among children. By fostering an atmosphere of inclusivity, acceptance, and love, we create a space where children can experience the beauty of a Christian community.

The impact of these friendships and connections in Kidmin is profound. Children who experience genuine friendship and a sense of belonging are more likely to thrive in their faith. They become more engaged, enthusiastic, and committed to their journey with Jesus. They are encouraged to grow in their understanding of God's Word, develop their spiritual gifts, and impact their world with the love and truth of Christ.

Heavenly Father, we thank You for the gift of community and friendship within Kidmin. We pray for the children in our care, asking that You would bless them with meaningful friendships and connections. Help us, as Kidmin leaders, to create an environment where children feel valued, accepted, and loved. May the friendships formed in Kidmin be a source of encouragement, growth, and joy in their lives. In Jesus' name, we pray. Amen.

Takeaway

Kidmin matters deeply because it provides opportunities for children to experience the beauty of community and friendship. Within the supportive Christian environment of children's ministry, kids can form meaningful connections with their peers and develop lifelong friendships. They also have the chance to connect with caring mentors and leaders who can pour into their lives. Let us embrace the significance of community and friendship in Kidmin, knowing that these relationships can sharpen and strengthen children's faith, creating a sense of belonging and providing avenues for discipleship to flourish. IT MATTERS.

_____

_____

_____

_____

_____

_____

_____

_____

KIDS ARE NOT JUST
TOMORROW'S LEADERS;
THEY ARE
leaders today
IN GOD'S EYES.

WEEK 30 : IT MATTERS TO KIDS
Scripture as a Lifeline: Kidmin's Role in Equipping Vulnerable Kids with Hope

"The righteous cry out, and the LORD hears them; he delivers them from all their troubles. The LORD is close to the brokenhearted and saves those who are crushed in spirit."
Psalm 34:17-18

Kidmin matters deeply because it recognizes the importance of reaching out to the most vulnerable kids in our communities. Many children who come through the doors of our churches carry heavy burdens—whether it be the weight of abuse, anxiety, physical disabilities, or other challenges. As kidmin leaders, we have a unique opportunity to offer them the hope and support found in Scripture.

The words of Psalm 34:17-18 remind us of the compassionate nature of our Heavenly Father. These verses remind us that God is attentive to the cries of His children, especially those who are vulnerable and in need of His love and healing touch.

For many vulnerable kids, the home environment may not provide the safety, security, and support they desperately need. Some may have experienced emotional or physical abuse, while others may battle anxiety, fear, or physical disabilities. In the face of such challenges, the hope of Scripture becomes a beacon of light, guiding them through the darkest times.

Kidmin plays a pivotal role in offering hope and support to these vulnerable kids. Through intentional teaching and discipleship, we have the privilege of sharing the transformative power of the gospel. We provide them with a safe and loving environment where they can experience the unconditional love of Jesus and find solace in His promises.

The hope of Scripture speaks directly to the hearts of vulnerable kids. It assures them that God hears their cries and delivers them from their troubles. It reminds them that even in the midst of brokenness and despair, God is near, extending His comforting embrace. The promises of Scripture become a lifeline that these children can grasp onto, sustaining them through their darkest moments.

As kidmin leaders, we must be intentional in equipping these vulnerable kids with the truths of God's Word. We must ensure that every child who enters our doors leaves with Scripture and support that will carry them through their daily lives. Through creative teaching, engaging activities, and intentional discipleship, we create opportunities for these children to encounter the hope, love, and transformation found in Jesus Christ.

Moreover, Kidmin should be a place where vulnerable kids find acceptance, belonging, and a sense of family. By cultivating a community that is rooted in compassion, understanding, and unconditional love, we create an environment where these children can experience healing and restoration. We become the hands and feet of Jesus, demonstrating His love and care for them.

Heavenly Father, we thank You for the opportunity to minister to the most vulnerable kids through Kidmin. We lift up these precious children to You, knowing that You hear their cries and are close to the brokenhearted. We ask for Your healing touch to be upon them, granting them comfort, strength, and hope found in Your Word. Help us, as Kidmin leaders, to provide the support and love these children desperately need. May they encounter Your transforming power and experience the joy of belonging to Your family. In Jesus' name, we pray. Amen.

Takeaway

Kidmin matters deeply because it offers hope and support to the most vulnerable kids. Through intentional teaching, discipleship, and a nurturing environment, we have the privilege of sharing the hope of Scripture and demonstrating the love of Jesus to these children. Let us be steadfast in our commitment to providing them with the necessary support, guidance, and encouragement that will carry them through their daily lives. May the hope of Scripture be a beacon of light, leading these vulnerable kids to experience healing, restoration, and the transformative power of God's love. IT MATTERS.

_____

_____

_____

_____

_____

_____

_____

_____

IN CHILDREN'S MINISTRY,
WE ARE BUILDING A
spiritual family
THAT SPANS GENERATIONS.

WEEK 31 : IT MATTERS TO KIDS
Fun with a Purpose: Why Kidmin Matters in Age-Appropriate Learning

"I gave you milk, not solid food, for you were not yet ready for it.
Indeed, you are still not ready."
1 Corinthians 3:2

Kidmin matters deeply because it recognizes the importance of providing age-appropriate learning experiences for children. Children's ministry utilizes engaging and interactive methods to teach children about God at their development level, making the learning process fun, accessible, and impactful.

The verse in 1 Corinthians 3:2 offers valuable insight into the concept of age-appropriate learning. Paul recognizes that spiritual growth and understanding happen progressively, just as physical and cognitive development occurs in stages.

Kidmin plays a vital role in meeting children where they are developmental. It offers a curriculum and teaching methods tailored to their age, allowing them to grasp biblical truths in a way that resonates with their young hearts and minds. By providing age-appropriate learning experiences, we create an environment where children can engage with God's Word, ask questions, and grow in their faith journey.

One of the strengths of children's ministry is its ability to present complex spiritual concepts in a way that children can understand. Through interactive lessons, hands-on activities, storytelling, and age-appropriate resources, Kidmin captures children's attention and helps them grasp foundational truths about God, Jesus, the Bible, and the principles of the Christian faith.

By utilizing creative teaching methods, Kidmin ensures that learning about God is not just educational but also enjoyable. Whether it's through crafts, games, songs, or dramatic presentations, children are actively involved in the learning process. This engagement enhances their comprehension, retention, and application of biblical truths.

Age-appropriate learning in Kidmin not only focuses on cognitive development but also nurtures children's spiritual and emotional growth. It creates a safe space where they can explore their faith, express their thoughts and emotions, and build a personal connection with God. Children are encouraged to ask questions, share their experiences, and engage in meaningful discussions that foster a deeper understanding of their relationship with God.

The impact of age-appropriate learning in Kidmin is significant. When children have the opportunity to learn about God in a manner that aligns with their developmental stage, they are more likely to embrace their faith, grow in their knowledge of God's Word, and develop a lifelong love for learning about Him. Kidmin sets a foundation for spiritual growth, preparing children for the next stages of their faith journey.

Heavenly Father, we thank You for the gift of age-appropriate learning in Kidmin. We pray for the children in our care, asking that You guide us as we teach and nurture them. Grant us wisdom and creativity to present biblical truths in a way that resonates with their hearts and minds. May the learning experiences in Kidmin ignite a passion for knowing You and lead them to a lifelong pursuit of a vibrant relationship with You. In Jesus' name, we pray. Amen.

Takeaway

Kidmin matters deeply because it provides age-appropriate learning experiences for children. By utilizing engaging and interactive teaching methods, Kidmin ensures that children can grasp biblical truths at their developmental level. Let us appreciate the significance of age-appropriate learning, recognizing that it creates a foundation for children's spiritual growth and sets them on a path of lifelong learning about God. IT MATTERS.

_____

_____

_____

_____

_____

_____

_____

_____

CHILDREN'S MINISTRY
IS WHERE THE

seeds of faith

BLOSSOM INTO BEAUTIFUL
FLOWERS OF DEVOTION.

WEEK 32 : IT MATTERS TO KIDS
Raising World Changers: Why Kidmin's Focus on Character Matters

"Be kind and compassionate to one another, forgiving each other,
just as in Christ God forgave you."
Ephesians 4:32

Kidmin matters deeply because it recognizes the importance of character development in children. Through children's ministry, kids have the opportunity to learn and internalize values such as love, kindness, honesty, forgiveness, and respect. These godly character traits shape their lives, guiding their decisions and interactions with others.

The verse in Ephesians 4:32 beautifully captures the essence of godly character development. This verse highlights the importance of cultivating character traits that reflect the love and forgiveness we have received from God through Jesus Christ.

Kidmin plays a vital role in instilling these character traits in children. Through intentional teaching, role modeling, and engaging activities, children's ministry creates an environment where godly values are taught, practiced, and internalized. By consistently emphasizing love, kindness, honesty, forgiveness, and respect, Kidmin equips children with the tools they need to navigate life with integrity and grace.

The values children learn in Kidmin have a transformative impact on their lives. Love becomes the foundation of their relationships, guiding their interactions with family, friends, and strangers. Kindness becomes their default response, enabling them to extend compassion and support to those in need. Honesty becomes a core value, fostering trust and integrity in their words and actions. Forgiveness becomes a natural inclination, promoting healing and reconciliation. Respect becomes a guiding principle, helping them honor and value the worth of every individual.

Character development through Kidmin goes beyond teaching children about right and wrong. It seeks to transform their hearts, empowering them to become more like Christ. As children embrace these godly character traits, they not only experience personal growth but also become beacons of light in their communities, shining God's love and grace to those around them.

In the context of Kidmin, character development occurs through intentional teaching and reinforcement. Children engage in activities that promote empathy, teamwork, and problem-solving skills. They participate in discussions that encourage critical thinking and reflection. They witness positive examples of character in their leaders and peers. Through these experiences, they learn not only the "what" but also the "why" behind godly character.

The impact of character development in Kidmin extends far beyond childhood. As children grow into adolescence and adulthood, the character traits they have cultivated in Kidmin become the guiding principles that shape their choices, relationships, and contributions to society. These godly values empower them to positively impact their families, schools, workplaces, and communities.

Heavenly Father, we thank You for the opportunity to shape godly character in children through Kidmin. We pray that as children engage in this ministry, they would grow in love, kindness, honesty, forgiveness, and respect. Help us, as Kidmin leaders, to model these character traits and teach them with wisdom and grace. May the character developed in Kidmin positively impact children's lives and inspire them to live out Your values in all they do. In Jesus' name, we pray. Amen.

Takeaway

Kidmin matters deeply because it fosters character development in children. Through intentional teaching, role modeling, and engaging activities, Kidmin equips children with godly character traits that positively impact their lives. Let us appreciate the significance of character development in Kidmin, recognizing that it shapes children's choices, relationships, and contributions to society. May the values learned in Kidmin empower children to be a reflection of Christ's love, kindness, honesty, forgiveness, and respect in the world. IT MATTERS.

_____

_____

_____

_____

_____

_____

_____

_____

KIDS ARE NOT JUST
RECEIVERS OF LOVE;
THEY ARE

givers

OF LOVE TOO.

WEEK 33 : IT MATTERS TO KIDS
Worship with Wonder: Why Kidmin Matters in Encouraging Kids to Praise

Worship the LORD with gladness; come before him with joyful songs."
Psalm 100:2

Kidmin matters deeply because it introduces children to the transformative power of worship and prayer. Through children's ministry, kids learn how to express their love for God, engage in heartfelt worship, and communicate with Him personally through prayer.

The verse in Psalm 100:2 encourages us to worship the Lord with gladness and come before Him with joyful songs. This verse captures the essence of a vibrant and personal relationship with God, where worship and prayer become integral aspects of our lives. Kidmin plays a significant role in laying the foundation for children to experience the richness of worship and prayer.

Children's ministry introduces kids to worship, teaching them how to express their love for God through music, songs, and actions. It provides opportunities for them to engage in heartfelt worship, lifting their voices and hearts to God. Through interactive and age-appropriate worship experiences, Kidmin allows children to encounter God's presence, fostering a deep sense of connection and reverence.

Worship in Kidmin is more than singing songs. It is about cultivating a genuine and personal relationship with God. As children engage in worship, they learn to express their gratitude, awe, and adoration for God's love and goodness. They discover the joy of celebrating who God is and what He has done. Through worship, children are encouraged to bring their praises, hopes, and fears before the throne of grace.

Prayer is another essential aspect of children's ministry. Kidmin teaches children the power of prayer and guides them in developing a personal relationship with God through conversation with Him. Children learn that prayer is not just a religious duty but a privilege—a direct line of communication with their Heavenly Father.

In Kidmin, children are taught that prayer is not limited to specific times or places but is a constant dialogue with God. They learn to share their joys, concerns, and needs with Him, knowing that He listens and cares for them. Through interactive prayer activities, children experience the comfort, peace, and guidance that come from seeking God's presence and inviting Him into their lives.

Kidmin empowers children to understand that worship and prayer are not confined to a church building or a specific age group. It is a lifestyle that can be lived out wherever they go. As they grow in their understanding of worship and prayer, children become ambassadors of God's love, carrying His presence and sharing it with others in their homes, schools, and communities.

The impact of worship and prayer in Kidmin is profound. It shapes children's spiritual lives, fostering a deep love for God and a desire to know Him intimately. As children engage in worship and prayer, their faith is strengthened, their hearts are transformed, and they develop a lifelong habit of seeking God's presence in all aspects of their lives.

Heavenly Father, we thank You for the privilege of worship and prayer in Kidmin. We pray that as children engage in these practices, their hearts would be filled with joy and reverence for You. Help us, as Kidmin leaders, to guide children in developing a personal relationship with You through worship and prayer. May they experience the transformative power of these spiritual disciplines and grow in their love and devotion to You. In Jesus' name, we pray. Amen.

Takeaway

Kidmin matters deeply because it introduces children to the transformative power of worship and prayer. Through engaging and age-appropriate experiences, Kidmin empowers children to express their love for God, engage in heartfelt worship, and develop a personal relationship with Him through prayer. Let us value the significance of worship and prayer in Kidmin, recognizing that they shape children's spiritual lives, foster a deep connection with God, and empower them to live out their faith beyond the walls of the church. IT MATTERS.

IN CHILDREN'S MINISTRY,
WE ARE

passing the baton

OF FAITH FROM
ONE GENERATION
TO THE NEXT.

WEEK 34 : IT MATTERS TO KIDS
Invited to the King's Table

"Therefore welcome one another as Christ has welcomed you,
for the glory of God."
Romans 15:7

In the bustling world of today, there's a particular group that often goes unnoticed, a group that's dear to the heart of God—kids who are at risk, overlooked, and sometimes forgotten. Just as King David extended an unexpected invitation to Mephibosheth, a forgotten prince, we are called to reach out to these precious ones and welcome them into the vibrant tapestry of Kidmin.

In 2 Samuel 9, we encounter a powerful story that mirrors the heart of God for these children. Mephibosheth, the grandson of Saul, had experienced brokenness and loss. With his physical disability and royal lineage, he had every reason to believe he would remain forgotten, even shunned. But King David, driven by compassion, searched for him and invited him to his table.

Just like Mephibosheth, the kids at risk whom we serve often carry burdens of their own. They might feel broken, unimportant, or isolated. But we have the opportunity to emulate King David's heart, to actively seek them out, and invite them into our Kidmin "table" of love, acceptance, and belonging.

Through engaging lessons, attentive listening, and intentional relationships, we can help them discover their unique value in God's eyes. Our Kidmin can become a place where they find refuge from life's challenges, where they experience God's unconditional love, and where they understand that they are never forgotten in His sight.

Dear Lord, thank You for reminding us of the profound significance of every child, especially those who are at risk and forgotten. Just as You reached out to Mephibosheth, inspire us to extend our hands of love and acceptance to these precious ones. Help us create a safe space where they can experience Your grace and healing. Guide us to mirror Your heart and ensure that no child feels left out or alone. In Jesus' name, we pray. Amen.

Takeaway

Let's remember that every child matters deeply to God. Just as King David's gesture changed Mephibosheth's life, our efforts in Kidmin can be transformative for kids who are at risk. Through our intentional love, attention, and compassion, we can bring them into the warmth of God's family. Let's actively seek out these kids, extend a hand of friendship, and invite them to the table where they can experience the fullness of God's love and acceptance. Our actions might impact their lives more profoundly than we can imagine.

_____

_____

_____

_____

_____

_____

_____

_____

CHILDREN'S MINISTRY
IS LIKE A LIGHTHOUSE

guiding young hearts

TO THE SAFE HARBOR
OF GOD'S LOVE.

WEEK 35 : IT MATTERS TO KIDS
Knowing Whose I Am: Kidmin's Impact on Building Children's Identity

"I praise you because I am fearfully and wonderfully made; your works are wonderful, I know that full well."
Psalm 139:14

Kidmin matters deeply because it offers children a safe and encouraging environment where they feel valued, supported, and affirmed in their identity as children of God. In today's culture, where children face various challenges and pressures, it is essential for them to be rooted in their identity as God's beloved and purposefully created individuals.

The words of Psalm 139 remind us that each child is fearfully and wonderfully made by God. Kidmin plays a crucial role in helping children understand and embrace their identity as unique and cherished individuals, created with purpose and intention.

In today's culture, children are bombarded with messages that can undermine their sense of self-worth and identity. They may face comparisons, societal expectations, and pressures that challenge their confidence and self-esteem. Kidmin provides a counter-narrative, where children are surrounded by loving leaders and volunteers who affirm their value and worth in God's eyes.

Children's ministry leaders and volunteers create an environment where children feel accepted, loved, and supported for who they are. They speak words of encouragement, highlighting each child's unique strengths and gifts. Through their actions and words, Kidmin leaders affirm children's identity as children of God, reminding them that they are deeply loved and cherished by their Heavenly Father.

Kidmin also plays a vital role in instilling a strong foundation of faith and identity in children. Through age-appropriate teaching and discussions, children learn about their identity as children of God and the truth that he intentionally created them. They are taught that their worth is not defined by external factors but by the unconditional love and grace of God.

In children's ministry, children are encouraged to embrace their purpose and gifts. They are inspired to discover and develop their unique talents, knowing that they have a significant role to play in God's kingdom. Kidmin provides opportunities for children to explore their passions, serve others, and use their gifts to make a positive impact in their families, communities, and beyond.

The encouragement and support children receive in Kidmin are transformative. When children experience an environment where they are valued and affirmed, it builds their confidence, self-esteem, and resilience. It empowers them to face challenges with courage, knowing that they are not alone but surrounded by a community that believes in them and supports them.

Kidmin's role in providing encouragement and support goes beyond the walls of the church. The impact extends into children's daily lives, empowering them to navigate the complexities of the world with a sense of identity, purpose, and God's love as their guiding compass.

Heavenly Father, we thank You for the gift of Kidmin and the encouragement and support it provides to children. We pray that as children engage in this ministry, they would deeply know and embrace their identity as fearfully and wonderfully made by You. Help us, as Kidmin leaders, to create a loving and affirming environment where children feel valued and supported. May they grow in confidence, knowing that they are loved by You and have a unique purpose in Your kingdom. In Jesus' name, we pray. Amen.

Takeaway

Kidmin matters deeply because it offers children a loving and encouraging environment where they feel valued, supported, and affirmed in their identity as children of God. Let us recognize the significance of providing encouragement and support to children, particularly in a culture that challenges their self-worth. Through Kidmin, may children embrace their identity, knowing that they are fearfully and wonderfully made by God and created with a purpose. May they experience the transformative power of love, encouragement, and support, empowering them to navigate life with confidence and grace. IT MATTERS.

_____

_____

_____

_____

_____

_____

_____

_____

_____

KIDS ARE NOT
JUST STUDENTS; THEY ARE

carriers

OF GOD'S TRUTH.

WEEK 36 : IT MATTERS TO KIDS
Tackling the Tough Stuff: Why Kidmin's Support in Answering Kids' Questions is Essential

"Your word is a lamp for my feet, a light on my path."
Psalm 119:105

Kidmin matters deeply because it provides a safe space for children to seek answers to tough real-life questions. In today's culture, children are exposed to various challenges and uncertainties that can leave them feeling confused and fearful. However, as Kidmin leaders, we have the opportunity to guide them with the truth of Scripture.

The verse in Psalm 119:105 reminds us that God's Word is a lamp for our feet and a light on our path. In a world filled with uncertainties, children need a solid foundation, and Kidmin plays a vital role in providing them with answers to tough questions. It offers them a safe and nurturing environment where they can explore and understand the timeless wisdom and guidance found in Scripture.

Today's culture can be intimidating, presenting children with challenging questions about morality, identity, relationships, and more. As Kidmin leaders, we have the responsibility to help children navigate these complexities and find biblical perspectives. We should encourage them to bring their hard questions, doubts, and concerns, assuring them that God's Word has the answers they seek.

Children need to know that the Bible is not just a collection of ancient stories but a living and relevant guidebook for their lives today. Through age-appropriate teaching, discussions, and engaging activities, Kidmin leaders can help children discover how Scripture applies to their everyday experiences. They learn that God's Word addresses current topics, offering wisdom, comfort, and direction in the midst of their challenges.

One of the most impactful ways Kidmin can provide answers to tough questions is by demonstrating how Scripture speaks in real-life situations. Children should be encouraged to explore the Bible's teachings on various topics, such as friendship, forgiveness, honesty, and self-worth. By diving into these themes, children develop a biblical worldview that shapes their thinking and decision-making.

In Kidmin, we aim to create an atmosphere where children feel comfortable discussing their questions openly. We foster an environment of curiosity, ensuring that children know their inquiries are valued and respected. We can guide them to seek biblical truths, supporting their journey of discovering answers while emphasizing the importance of faith and trust in God's Word.

As we provide answers to tough questions, it is crucial to remain humble and acknowledge that we don't have all the answers. We can encourage children to explore the Bible for themselves, teaching them how to study and interpret Scripture with discernment. This empowers them to develop a personal relationship with God and engage in a lifelong pursuit of truth.

In Kidmin, our role is not only to provide answers but also to walk alongside children as they navigate their faith journey. We can point them to the ultimate source of wisdom, God Himself. Through prayer, Bible study, and seeking guidance from the Holy Spirit, children can grow in their understanding of God's Word and apply it to their lives.

Heavenly Father, we thank You for the gift of Your Word, which provides answers to our tough questions. We pray for the children in Kidmin who are seeking answers and grappling with the complexities of life. Guide us, as Kidmin leaders, to navigate these discussions with wisdom, grace, and humility. Help us point children to the truth found in the Scripture, empowering them to trust in Your Word and develop a firm foundation for their lives. In Jesus' name, we pray. Amen.

Takeaway

Kidmin matters deeply because it offers children a safe space to seek answers to tough real-life questions. By exploring Scripture and engaging in discussions, children can find guidance and wisdom for the challenges they face. Let us encourage children to bring their hard questions, assuring them that God's Word has relevance and answers for every aspect of their lives. As Kidmin leaders, may we guide children to develop a biblical worldview, empowering them to navigate the complexities of culture with confidence and truth. IT MATTERS.

_____

_____

_____

_____

_____

_____

_____

_____

_____

IN CHILDREN'S MINISTRY,
WE ARE
lighting the fire
OF PASSION FOR JESUS IN
LITTLE HEARTS.

WEEK 37 : IT MATTERS TO YOUR COMMUNITY AND THE WORLD
Building Bridges to the Gospel: Kidmin's Impact in Connecting Communities

"Jesus said, 'Let the little children come to me, and do not hinder them, for the kingdom of heaven belongs to such as these.'"
Matthew 19:14

Kidmin matters greatly to your community because it serves as a vital connection point to the church and, ultimately, the Gospel. In today's world, many individuals may be hesitant to attend a church service on a Sunday, but they are more likely to bring their children to special events like Vacation Bible School or Trunk or Treat. These intentional outreach endeavors create strategic opportunities to demonstrate love and present the hope of the Gospel to a community in need.

The verse in Matthew 19:14 reveals Jesus' heart for children. He understood the significance of children and their connection to the Kingdom of God. Likewise, Kidmin serves as a bridge, allowing children and their families to encounter the love of Jesus and the transformative power of the Gospel.

In your community, there may be individuals who are hesitant or reluctant to step foot into a church building. However, through Kidmin outreach events like Vacation Bible School (VBS), sports camp, or other engaging programs, you create a welcoming environment where families feel comfortable bringing their children. These events provide a non-threatening entry point, allowing families to experience the love and joy of the church community.

Kidmin serves as a strategic tool for connecting communities to the Gospel by intentionally building relationships with children and their families. It offers a safe space for children to have fun, make friends, and explore faith in age-appropriate ways. Through engaging activities, interactive teaching, and meaningful relationships with caring volunteers, children are introduced to the good news of Jesus.

Vacation Bible School, for example, becomes a week-long immersion into biblical teachings, music, games, and crafts. It offers an opportunity for children to learn about Jesus, experience His love, and build relationships with Christian mentors. These events not only impact the children but also create a positive impression on their parents and caregivers, fostering curiosity and openness to further engagement with the church community.

Kidmin outreach events also demonstrate God's love in tangible ways, such as providing resources for families in need, supporting local schools, or organizing community service projects. These efforts show that the church cares about the well-being of the community and seeks to meet practical needs while sharing the message of hope found in Christ.

As Kidmin leaders and volunteers, you have the privilege of being an ambassador of the Gospel, extending God's love beyond the church walls. Your dedication and passion for reaching out to the community have the power to transform lives. By offering an inclusive, loving, and Christ-centered environment, you create a connection point for families who may be searching for something more in their lives.

Through these outreach events, families begin to experience the warmth of the church community, witness the authenticity of Christian relationships, and encounter the life-changing message of the Gospel. Seeds of faith are planted, relationships are formed, and lives are touched by the transformative power of Jesus.

Heavenly Father, we thank You for the opportunities Kidmin provides to connect communities to the Gospel. We pray for wisdom, creativity, and compassion as we engage with families in our community. May our outreach events be filled with love, joy, and the transformative message of the Gospel. Open hearts and minds to receive Your love and truth. May the seeds planted through Kidmin grow into a flourishing faith and a vibrant relationship with You. In Jesus' name, we pray. Amen.

Takeaway

Kidmin matters greatly to your community because it serves as a connection point to the church and the Gospel. Through intentional outreach events, families are drawn in, experiencing the love and joy of the church community. As Kidmin leaders and volunteers, embrace the opportunity to build relationships, demonstrate God's love, and share the hope found in Jesus. May your efforts create a ripple effect, transforming lives and communities for the glory of God. IT MATTERS.

_____

_____

_____

_____

_____

_____

_____

_____

_____

CHILDREN'S MINISTRY
IS WHERE

young dreams

ARE TRANSFORMED
INTO GOD'S DIVINE PLANS.

WEEK 38 : IT MATTERS TO YOUR COMMUNITY AND THE WORLD
Love in Action: Why Kidmin Matters for At-Risk Kids in Our Community

"Religion that God our Father accepts as pure and faultless is this: to look after orphans and widows in their distress and to keep oneself from being polluted by the world."
James 1:27

Kidmin matters deeply to your community because it allows us to care for the most at-risk kids. As followers of Jesus, we are called to be His hands and feet, showing love, compassion, and support to those who are vulnerable. When churches embody this calling, we become beacons of hope and strength in our communities.

The verse in James 1:27 reminds us of the essence of true religion - to look after orphans and widows in their distress. While the specific mention of orphans and widows applies to a particular group, the underlying principle extends to all those who are vulnerable, including at-risk children in our communities. Kidmin offers a unique opportunity to demonstrate Jesus' love by providing care and support to those who need it most.

In our communities, there are children facing various challenges and hardships. Some may come from broken homes, unstable family situations, or have experienced trauma. These at-risk kids need a place where they can find stability, love, and support. Kidmin becomes a safe haven, a sanctuary where they can experience the nurturing care of God's people.

As Kidmin leaders and volunteers, we have the privilege of being the hands and feet of Jesus to these precious children. We can offer practical assistance, emotional support, and spiritual guidance to help them navigate the difficulties they face. By demonstrating Jesus' love in action, we provide a tangible expression of God's compassion and care.

Jesus Himself exemplified this holistic approach to ministry during His time on earth. He not only addressed people's spiritual needs but also cared for their physical well-being. He fed the hungry, healed the sick, and comforted the broken-hearted. As His followers, we are called to follow in His footsteps, extending love and support to those in need.

Through Kidmin, we can meet the physical needs of at-risk children by providing nutritious meals, access to resources, and opportunities for healthcare and well-being. Additionally, we have the privilege of addressing their spiritual needs by sharing the message of God's love, teaching them about Jesus, and helping them grow in their faith.

It is essential to remember that caring for at-risk kids extends beyond the walls of the church. We must partner with other organizations, community groups, and families to provide comprehensive support. By working collaboratively, we can offer a network of care that meets the diverse needs of these vulnerable children.

As Kidmin leaders, we have the responsibility to create an environment of love, acceptance, and belonging. We can foster a culture of inclusion where every child feels valued and embraced for who they are. By building genuine relationships, listening to their stories, and offering a supportive community, we become a source of strength and hope in their lives.

Heavenly Father, we thank You for Your heart of compassion and care for the most vulnerable. We pray for the at-risk kids in our communities that You would surround them with love, protection, and support. Guide us, as Kidmin leaders, to be instruments of Your love, extending a helping hand and a listening ear to those in need. Use us to bring healing, hope, and transformation in their lives. In Jesus' name, we pray. Amen.

Takeaway

Kidmin matters greatly to your community because it enables us to care for the most at-risk kids. By extending love, compassion, and support, we can make a significant impact in their lives. As Kidmin leaders and volunteers, let us embody Jesus' example of holistic ministry, addressing both the physical and spiritual needs of these vulnerable children. Together, we can create an environment where they feel safe, valued, and surrounded by God's love. IT MATTERS.

_____

_____

_____

_____

_____

_____

_____

_____

KIDS ARE NOT JUST
THE CHURCH OF TOMORROW;
THEY ARE VITAL MEMBERS
OF THE
family of God
TODAY.

WEEK 39 : IT MATTERS TO YOUR COMMUNITY AND THE WORLD
Raising Kidmin Warriors: Empowering Kids for Mission in Your Community

"You are the light of the world. A town built on a hill cannot be hidden. Neither do people light a lamp and put it under a bowl. Instead, they put it on its stand, and it gives light to everyone in the house. In the same way, let your light shine before others, that they may see your good deeds and glorify your Father in heaven."
Matthew 5:14-16

Kidmin matters deeply to your community because our children are a mighty mission force. Every week, as we send our kids out from the church, they enter various spheres of influence that serve as their mission field. Whether it's school, sports practice, the library, or a friend's house, these are opportunities for them to show the love of Christ and share the truth of Scripture. As Kidmin leaders, it is our responsibility to equip and empower our kids to be effective ambassadors for Christ in their daily lives.

In the scripture passage from Matthew 5:14-16, Jesus declares, "You are the light of the world." He emphasizes that as His followers, we are called to be a shining beacon in a world that desperately needs the light of His love and truth. This calling extends to our children, who have the unique opportunity to be light-bearers in their communities.

As kidmin leaders, we have the privilege and responsibility to prepare our kids each week to be mission-minded and ready to share the love of Christ wherever they go. We are equipping them to let their light shine brightly before others so they may see their good deeds and glorify our Father in heaven.

Our children enter their mission field each day surrounded by classmates, friends, and neighbors who may not yet know Jesus. These interactions provide significant opportunities for them to demonstrate the love of Christ through their words, actions, and attitudes. When they display kindness, forgiveness, and compassion, they become living testimonies of God's grace and draw others closer to Him.

Kidmin plays a vital role in mobilizing children as a mighty mission force by teaching them the foundational truths of Scripture and equipping them with practical tools to share their faith. Through engaging lessons, interactive discussions, and meaningful activities, we help our kids understand their identity in Christ and how to live out their faith in their communities.

We teach them to pray for their friends, classmates, and neighbors so that they may come to know Jesus personally. We encourage them to invite others to church events or share Bible stories that have impacted their lives. We equip them with age-appropriate resources, like Scripture memory verses or gospel tracts, that they can easily share with those around them.

Furthermore, we instill in them a sense of responsibility and ownership in fulfilling the Great Commission. We help them grasp the significance of their role as ambassadors for Christ, empowering them to be intentional in their interactions, to listen with empathy, and to speak words of truth and encouragement.

As our children become more engaged in their mission field, we witness the transformative power of the Gospel at work. Seeds of faith are planted, lives are impacted, and communities are touched by the love of Christ. The simple acts of kindness, heartfelt prayers, and genuine conversations with our children can have a profound ripple effect in their circles of influence.

Heavenly Father, we thank You for the privilege of mobilizing our children as a mighty mission force. We pray that You would ignite a passion for sharing Your love in their hearts. Equip them with wisdom, boldness, and compassion as they interact with others. May their lives shine brightly as a reflection of Your love, drawing others to a personal relationship with Jesus. Use them to transform lives, families, and communities for Your glory. In Jesus' name, we pray. Amen.

Takeaway

Kidmin matters greatly to your community because it mobilizes children as a mighty mission force. Through intentional discipleship and equipping, our kids become ambassadors for Christ in their everyday lives. Let us continue to invest in their spiritual growth, teaching them to let their light shine brightly so that others may see their good deeds and glorify our Father in heaven. Together, let us raise up a generation of children who impact their communities for the Kingdom of God. IT MATTERS.

_____

_____

_____

_____

_____

_____

_____

_____

_____

IN CHILDREN'S MINISTRY,
WE HAVE THE

joy

OF SEEING YOUNG LIVES
TRANSFORMED BY
GOD'S GRACE.

WEEK 40 : IT MATTERS TO YOUR COMMUNITY AND THE WORLD
Sprinkling Love: Why Kidmin Matters as Salt in Our Communities

"You are the salt of the earth. But if the salt loses its saltiness, how can it be made salty again? It is no longer good for anything, except to be thrown out and trampled underfoot."
Matthew 5:13

Kidmin matters deeply to your community because it serves as salt in a world that needs it. Each church is a beacon of light shining in the area where God has placed it. Our kids who attend our weekly services become little salt shakers as they go out and season the world with God's love. Salt is desperately needed in situations where kindness can bring hope, where forgiveness can diffuse anger, and where truth can guide the way. The salt our kids bring to their daily interactions is changing their worlds.

In Matthew 5:13, Jesus tells His disciples, "You are the salt of the earth." In biblical times, salt was a precious commodity with various uses. It preserved food, added flavor, and acted as a purifying agent. Similarly, as followers of Jesus, we are called to be salt in the world around us, bringing preservation, flavor, and purity through our words and actions.

Kidmin plays a crucial role in cultivating this salt-like quality in our children. Through engaging teaching, discipleship, and mentorship, we empower them to be influencers in their communities. Our kids are equipped with the truth of God's Word, which becomes the foundation for their actions and interactions with others.

As they go out into their schools, neighborhoods, and extracurricular activities, our kids have the opportunity to be salt in situations that desperately need it. They can bring kindness to a hurting classmate, forgiveness to a friend who has made a mistake, and truth to those who are searching for guidance.

Just as salt enhances the flavor of food, our children can bring positivity and joy into their environments. Their words of encouragement, acts of kindness, and genuine care can significantly impact those they interact with. By being salt, they have the power to uplift spirits, restore hope, and make a lasting difference.

Moreover, salt acts as a preservative, keeping things from spoiling or decaying. In a world filled with negativity, our children can bring a fresh perspective that counters despair and brokenness. They can promote unity, reconciliation, and love, standing against the decay of division and hatred.

However, it is crucial for our kids to maintain their saltiness. Jesus warns that if the salt loses its saltiness, it becomes useless. Similarly, if our children compromise their values or conform to the ways of the world, they lose their effectiveness in being salt. Kidmin must provide a solid foundation of biblical truth, discipleship, and accountability to help our kids stay true to their faith and their calling as salt-bearers.

Heavenly Father, we thank You for calling us to be salt in the world. We pray for our children who are attending Kidmin that You would empower them to be effective salt-shakers in their communities. Fill them with Your love, wisdom, and compassion as they interact with others. Help them to be a positive influence, bringing flavor, preservation, and purity wherever they go. May their lives reflect Your goodness and draw others to Your Kingdom. In Jesus' name, we pray. Amen.

Takeaway

Kidmin matters greatly to your community because it empowers children to be salt in a needy world. Through biblical teaching and discipleship, we equip our kids to bring flavor, preservation, and purity to their surroundings. Let us encourage and support them in being positive influencers, making a lasting impact through acts of kindness, forgiveness, and truth. Together, as the salt of the earth, we can bring hope, restoration, and the love of Christ to a world that desperately needs it. IT MATTERS.

_____

_____

_____

_____

_____

_____

_____

_____

CHILDREN'S MINISTRY
IS A CANVAS WHERE
God's masterpieces
ARE PAINTED
WITH LOVE AND CARE.

WEEK 41 : IT MATTERS TO YOUR COMMUNITY AND THE WORLD
Changing the Game: How Kidmin Tackles Social Issues Head-On

"Train up a child in the way he should go;
even when he is old he will not depart from it."
Proverbs 22:6

Kidmin matters deeply to our communities because it plays a crucial role in addressing prevalent social issues that children face. In today's world, children encounter challenges such as bullying, peer pressure, substance abuse, and mental health struggles. Children's ministry provides a safe and nurturing environment to equip children with the tools and knowledge needed to navigate these issues and make positive choices.

Proverbs 22:6 teaches us the importance of training up a child in the way they should go. As Kidmin leaders, we have the unique opportunity to come alongside children and guide them through the challenges they may face in society. By addressing social issues in a biblical context, we empower children to make informed decisions and live out their faith in practical ways.

Bullying is a prevalent social issue that affects many children. Kidmin can provide a safe space where children can learn about kindness, empathy, and standing up against injustice. By teaching children about biblical principles of love, forgiveness, and treating others with respect, we equip them to combat bullying with godly character and compassion.

Peer pressure is another significant challenge that children encounter. Through children's ministry, we can teach children the importance of making wise choices and standing firm in their faith. By empowering them to say no to negative influences and encouraging healthy friendships, we help them navigate peer pressure with confidence and integrity.

Substance abuse is a growing concern, even among young children. Kidmin can address this issue by teaching children about the importance of taking care of their bodies as temples of the Holy Spirit. By instilling values of identities based on who God says we are, healthy habits, and the dangers of substance abuse, we equip children to make wise choices that honor God and protect their well-being.

Mental health is another critical social issue affecting children today. Kidmin can provide a nurturing environment where children can openly discuss their feelings, fears, and struggles. By promoting emotional well-being, sharing the hope of the gospel, and offering support and encouragement, we help children develop resilience and find hope in challenging times.

Addressing social issues in children's ministry goes beyond mere education. It involves building relationships, fostering empathy, and modeling Christ-like behavior. As we teach children about God's love, we show them how to extend that love to others who are hurting or in need. By promoting a culture of inclusivity, acceptance, and understanding, we create an environment where children can flourish and impact their communities positively.

Heavenly Father, we thank You for the privilege of serving children through Kidmin. We pray for wisdom and discernment as we address social issues affecting our communities. Help us teach children biblical values that equip them to make positive choices and navigate challenges with courage and faith. Grant us the ability to create a safe and nurturing environment where children can find healing, hope, and love. In Jesus' name, we pray. Amen.

Takeaway

Kidmin matters greatly to our communities because it addresses social issues that children face. Through biblical teaching, guidance, and mentorship, we empower children to navigate challenges such as bullying, peer pressure, substance abuse, and mental health struggles. Let us commit to equipping children with the tools and knowledge they need to make positive choices, live out their faith, and become catalysts for change in their communities. Together, as we address social issues, we sow seeds of love, kindness, and godly character in the next generation, making a lasting impact on our communities. IT MATTERS.

_____

_____

_____

_____

_____

_____

_____

_____

KIDS ARE NOT JUST SEEKERS;
THEY ARE

finders of truth

IN JESUS.

WEEK 42 : IT MATTERS TO YOUR COMMUNITY AND THE WORLD
Kids with a Global Heart:
Why Kidmin Matters to the World

"Go therefore and make disciples of all nations, baptizing them in the name of the Father and of the Son and of the Holy Spirit, teaching them to observe all that I have commanded you.
And behold, I am with you always, to the end of the age."
Matthew 28:19-20

Kidmin matters greatly to the world because it plays a crucial role in addressing global challenges. Children's ministry has the power to raise awareness among children about global issues such as poverty, hunger, and access to education. Most importantly, it helps children understand that there are kids around the world who have not heard the life-changing message of the gospel. By educating and empowering children, they can become advocates for change and actively contribute to addressing these issues in their communities and beyond.

In Matthew 28:19-20, Jesus gives the Great Commission, instructing His disciples to go and make disciples of all nations. This command extends to us today, including the youngest members of our churches. Kidmin plays a vital role in fulfilling this mission by raising awareness among children about global challenges and inspiring them to take action.

Children's ministry can educate children about global issues such as poverty, hunger, and lack of access to education. By teaching them about the realities faced by children around the world, we foster empathy and compassion in their hearts. They begin to understand that they can make a difference, no matter how small, in the lives of others.

Moreover, Kidmin has the opportunity to instill a global perspective in children. By highlighting the importance of reaching the unreached with the gospel, we expand their understanding of the world and its diverse cultures. We teach them that their faith is not limited to their local church but has the power to impact lives globally.

Empowering children to become advocates for change is another crucial aspect of Kidmin's role in addressing global challenges. We can teach children about the power of prayer and intercession for those in need. By encouraging them to pray for children around the world and supporting missionary efforts, we instill a heart for missions in their young lives.

Children can actively contribute to addressing global challenges by participating in service projects, fundraisers, and mission trips. These experiences provide opportunities for hands-on involvement and help children realize their capacity to make a tangible impact in the world. As they engage in these activities, they begin to understand the importance of reaching out to others with the love and message of Christ.

As we equip children to address global challenges, we are not merely creating a generation of socially conscious individuals. We are cultivating a generation of disciples who understand their role in the Great Commission. By teaching them to observe all that Jesus commanded, including love for their neighbors, they become ambassadors of the gospel, spreading the good news both locally and globally.

Heavenly Father, we thank You for the privilege of raising children in Kidmin who can address global challenges. Open their eyes to the needs of the world and give them hearts filled with compassion and love. Empower them to be advocates for change and ambassadors of the gospel. Guide them in making a tangible impact in the lives of others, both locally and globally. May they grow up with a deep passion for reaching the unreached and fulfilling the Great Commission. In Jesus' name, we pray. Amen.

Takeaway

Kidmin matters greatly to the world because it addresses global challenges by raising awareness, empowering children, and fostering a global perspective. By educating children about global issues, we cultivate empathy and compassion within them. As we empower them to take action, they become advocates for change and contribute to addressing these challenges in their communities and beyond. Let us guide our children to become ambassadors of the gospel, understanding their role in the Great Commission and spreading the love and message of Christ to the ends of the earth. Together, as Kidmin leaders and children, we can make a lasting impact on the world. IT MATTERS.

_____

_____

_____

_____

_____

_____

_____

_____

IN CHILDREN'S MINISTRY,
WE ARE CULTIVATING A

garden of faith

WHERE THE LOVE OF CHRIST
BLOOMS.

WEEK 43 : IT MATTERS TO YOUR COMMUNITY AND THE WORLD
Shaping Tomorrow's Leaders: The Impact of Children's Ministry

"We will not hide them from their descendants; we will tell the next generation the praiseworthy deeds of the Lord, his power, and the wonders he has done."
Psalm 78:4

Kidmin matters greatly to the world because it plays a vital role in training future global thinkers and leaders. Children's ministry provides a platform to pass down the faith to the next generation, ensuring that they are equipped with the knowledge of God's praiseworthy deeds, power, and wonders. By nurturing their faith and instilling a passion for God, we prepare children to make a kingdom impact on a global scale.

Psalm 78:4 emphasizes the importance of passing down the stories of God's faithfulness and power to the next generation. Children's ministry allows us to fulfill this vital role by teaching children about the praiseworthy deeds of the Lord, His power, and the wonders He has done. Through our discipleship and their relationship with Jesus, we empower them to become global thinkers and leaders.

As we share the stories of God's faithfulness and His mighty works, we inspire children to trust in His power and depend on Him in their lives. By recounting the accounts of how God has worked throughout history and in our own lives, we build their faith and instill in them a deep reverence for God. This foundation enables them to navigate the challenges of the world with confidence and hope.

Children's ministry also cultivates a heart for mission and compassion within children. By teaching them about the needs of others and the call to serve, we expand their worldview and help them develop empathy and a sense of responsibility towards others. We can expose them to global issues, encouraging them to pray, support, and actively engage in making a difference. Through these experiences, we raise children who are not only aware of the world's needs but also empowered to bring about positive change.

Moreover, Kidmin provides opportunities for children to develop essential leadership skills. By encouraging their participation in various activities, such as leading worship, serving in teams, and organizing events, we empower children to grow in their abilities to influence and inspire others. As they step into leadership roles within the ministry, they learn the importance of teamwork, communication, and serving with humility. These skills equip them to become effective leaders who can make a positive impact on a global scale.

In addition, children's ministry fosters a sense of community and collaboration among children. It creates an environment where they can connect with their peers, learn from one another, and build lifelong friendships. These relationships provide a support system that encourages and strengthens them as they navigate through life's challenges. By cultivating a sense of belonging, Kidmin helps children develop social and relational skills that are essential for building healthy relationships and collaborating with others in a global context.

Heavenly Father, we thank You for the privilege of training future global thinkers and leaders through Kidmin. Help us to faithfully share Your praiseworthy deeds, Your power, and the wonders You have done with the next generation. May their faith be grounded in Your faithfulness and their hearts filled with a passion for Your kingdom. Equip them with the necessary skills, compassion, and leadership abilities to make a positive impact on a global scale. May they shine brightly for Your glory and bring hope to a hurting world. In Jesus' name, we pray. Amen.

Takeaway

Kidmin matters greatly to the world because it plays a significant role in training future global thinkers and leaders. By sharing the stories of God's faithfulness, teaching compassion for others, developing leadership skills, and fostering a sense of community, we equip children to make a kingdom impact on a global scale. Let us faithfully impart the knowledge of God's praiseworthy deeds, His power, and the wonders He has done to the next generation. Together, through Kidmin, we are raising up a generation of global thinkers and leaders who will bring light, hope, and the transformative power of the gospel to the world. IT MATTERS.

_____

_____

_____

_____

_____

_____

_____

_____

_____

CHILDREN'S MINISTRY
IS WHERE YOUNG HANDS
LEARN TO

reach out

WITH KINDNESS
AND COMPASSION.

WEEK 44 : IT MATTERS TO YOUR COMMUNITY AND THE WORLD

From Here to Everywhere: Kidmin's Journey of Impacting the World

"But you will receive power when the Holy Spirit comes on you; and you will be
my witnesses in Jerusalem, and in all Judea and Samaria,
and to the ends of the earth."
Acts 1:8

Kidmin matters globally because it plays a vital role in missions and outreach efforts that extend beyond local communities. Children's ministry has the power to make a lasting global impact by spreading the love of Christ, sharing the gospel, and participating in mission initiatives.

Acts 1:8 records Jesus' instructions to His disciples before ascending to heaven. He promised them the Holy Spirit's power and commissioned them to be His witnesses not only in their immediate surroundings but also in "Jerusalem, and in all Judea and Samaria, and to the ends of the earth." These words apply to us as believers today and remind us of the importance of reaching out beyond our local communities to impact the world for Christ.

Children's ministry plays a crucial role in fulfilling this global mission. By teaching children about the love of Jesus and equipping them to be His witnesses, we empower them to become agents of transformation in their communities and beyond. As children learn about missions and outreach, they develop a heart for the world and a desire to share the good news of salvation with others.

Through mission initiatives, children's ministry provides opportunities for kids to actively engage in reaching the ends of the earth. Whether through supporting missionary efforts, participating in outreach projects, or praying for unreached people groups, children can be involved in fulfilling the Great Commission at an early age. By fostering a global perspective and nurturing a heart for missions, children's ministry sets the stage for a lifetime of kingdom impact.

Furthermore, Kidmin matters globally because it helps children understand the diverse needs and realities of the world. It exposes them to different cultures, languages, and customs, fostering empathy, understanding, and a sense of global citizenship. By broadening their worldview, children's ministry prepares kids to navigate an increasingly interconnected world with compassion, respect, and a Christ-centered perspective.

As children's ministry leaders, we have the privilege and responsibility to inspire children to embrace their role in global missions and outreach. We can teach them about the needs of unreached people groups, encourage them to pray for those who have never heard the gospel and equip them to be ambassadors of Christ's love. By instilling a passion for missions and a heart for the nations, we contribute to raising a generation that actively participates in God's global work.

Dear Heavenly Father, thank You for the privilege of being part of Your global mission through children's ministry. We ask for Your guidance and empowerment as we teach and equip children to be witnesses in their communities and to the ends of the earth. Ignite their hearts with a passion for missions and a deep love for those who have yet to hear the gospel. May our efforts in Kidmin contribute to fulfilling the Great Commission and advancing Your kingdom around the world. In Jesus' name, we pray. Amen.

Takeaway

Kidmin matters globally because it empowers children to be witnesses for Christ and actively participate in missions and outreach efforts. By nurturing a global perspective, teaching about diverse cultures, and instilling a passion for missions, children's ministry prepares the next generation to make a global impact. Let us continue to prioritize global missions in our Kidmin programs, trusting that God will use our efforts to reach the ends of the earth with His love and salvation. Together, through Kidmin, we can be a part of God's global mission to make disciples of all nations. IT MATTERS.

_____

_____

_____

_____

_____

_____

_____

_____

_____

KIDS ARE NOT
JUST FOLLOWERS;
they are leaders
OF FAITH AND LOVE.

WEEK 45 : IT MATTERS TO YOUR COMMUNITY AND THE WORLD

Title: Across Borders, One Heart: The Power of Global Kidmin Support

"Therefore encourage one another and build each other up,
just as in fact you are doing."
1 Thessalonians 5:11

Kidmin matters not just within our local communities but also on a global scale. Through the power of encouragement and support, we have the incredible opportunity to uplift our fellow Kidmin leaders and volunteers around the world.

As Kidmin leaders, we have experienced the impact of encouragement in our own ministries. A kind word, a listening ear, or a shared resource can make a significant difference. Imagine the power of our collective encouragement as we extend it beyond our local communities to our global Kidmin family.

The apostle Paul, in 1 Thessalonians 5:11, urges us to encourage one another and build each other up. This verse reminds us of the importance of fostering a culture of support and upliftment within the body of Christ. As part of the Kidmin community, we have a unique opportunity to extend this encouragement to our global counterparts.

One way we can support our global Kidmin family is by sharing our stories of God's faithfulness and the transformative impact of children's ministry. As we share our testimonies, we inspire and encourage others who may be facing similar challenges or seeking fresh ideas. Our stories become beacons of hope and sources of inspiration, reminding our global Kidmin family that they are not alone in their endeavors.

In addition to sharing stories, we can actively engage in mentorship and coaching relationships with fellow Kidmin leaders across the world. Through intentional connections, we can offer guidance, wisdom, and support to those who may be navigating unfamiliar territories or seeking to grow in their ministry skills. By investing in the development of our global Kidmin family, we contribute to the multiplication of effective and impactful children's ministries worldwide.

Furthermore, let us cultivate a spirit of unity and collaboration within our global Kidmin community. We can create platforms for sharing resources, ideas, and best practices, leveraging the power of technology to bridge the geographical divide. Through online forums, virtual conferences, and collaborative projects, we can build each other up, equipping one another for greater effectiveness in reaching children with the Gospel.

Dear Lord, we thank You for the privilege of being part of the global Kidmin family. Help us to encourage and build each other up, strengthening our bonds of unity and love. May our words and actions reflect Your heart of compassion and grace. We pray for our global Kidmin family that You would provide them with the wisdom, strength, and resources they need to impact children's lives for Your glory. Guide us in sharing our stories, offering mentorship, and fostering collaboration, so that together we may advance Your Kingdom through children's ministry. In Your name, we pray. Amen.

Takeaway

Kidmin matters globally because we have the opportunity to encourage and build up our fellow Kidmin leaders and volunteers around the world. Through the sharing of stories, mentorship, and collaboration, we can strengthen our global Kidmin family and inspire one another to reach new heights in ministry. Let us embrace our role in supporting and uplifting our global Kidmin community, knowing that together we can profoundly impact children's lives and advance God's Kingdom. As we encourage and build each other up, we reflect the love of Christ and demonstrate the power of unity in fulfilling our calling as Kidmin leaders. IT MATTERS.

_____

_____

_____

_____

_____

_____

_____

_____

IN CHILDREN'S MINISTRY,
WE ARE

nurturing hearts

THAT WILL

shine brightly

FOR JESUS.

WEEK 46 : IT MATTERS TO THE FUTURE

Sowing Faith, Reaping a Harvest: The Significance of Kidmin

"Let us not become weary in doing good, for at the proper time we will reap a harvest if we do not give up."
Galatians 6:9

Kidmin matters not only in the present but also for the future. As kidmin leaders, we have the incredible opportunity to sow seeds of faith, love, and discipleship into the lives of children.

The law of the harvest teaches us that we will reap what we sow. In the context of kidmin, this principle holds true as we invest in the lives of children, planting seeds of truth, love, and spiritual growth. Our efforts may not always bear immediate fruit, but as Galatians 6:9 reminds us, we are called to persevere and not grow weary in doing good.

When we faithfully teach children about God's love, His Word, and His plan for their lives, we are sowing seeds that will take root and grow. We may not see the full impact of our labor at the moment, but we can trust in the promise that a harvest will come at the proper time. The children we minister to today will carry the seeds we plant into their future, impacting their families, communities, and the world.

As we sow seeds of faith, we must also nurture and cultivate them through prayer, guidance, and intentional discipleship. We have the privilege of walking alongside children as they grow in their relationship with God, providing support and guidance to help them navigate life's challenges. Through consistent teaching, modeling Christ-like character, and fostering a vibrant community of faith, we prepare children for a future of walking with Jesus.

Moreover, Kidmin matters to the future because it equips children to become leaders and influencers in their spheres of influence. When children encounter Jesus and experience His transforming love, they are empowered to make a difference in their families, schools, and communities. Our investment in their spiritual growth has the potential to unleash a generation of young leaders who will impact the world for Christ.

Let us not underestimate the power of planting seeds in the lives of children: every Bible lesson, every prayer, and every act of love matters. We may not see immediate results, but we can have confidence that God is at work, nurturing our planted seeds and bringing forth a bountiful harvest in due time.

Heavenly Father, thank You for the privilege of serving in Kidmin and sowing seeds of faith into the lives of children. Help us not to grow weary in doing good, knowing that our labor is not in vain. We pray for the seeds we have planted to take root and grow, bearing fruit in the lives of the children we minister to. Give us wisdom, patience, and perseverance as we guide and disciple the future generation. May they become mighty ambassadors for Your Kingdom, impacting their families, communities, and the world. In Jesus' name, we pray. Amen.

Takeaway

Kidmin matters to the future because it involves sowing seeds of faith, love, and discipleship into the lives of children. Though we may not see immediate results, we can trust in the promise of a future harvest. Let us continue to invest in the spiritual growth of children, knowing that what we plant today will yield a bountiful harvest in due time. May we persevere in doing good, guided by the belief that God is at work, transforming hearts and raising up a generation of young leaders who will make a lasting impact for His Kingdom. IT MATTERS.

_____

_____

_____

_____

_____

_____

_____

_____

CHILDREN'S MINISTRY IS A
HARVEST FIELD WHERE

God's Love

REAPS A BOUNTIFUL CROP
OF SOULS.

WEEK 47 : IT MATTERS
TO THE FUTURE
The Ripple Effect: Kidmin and the Future Impact

"Cast your bread upon the waters, for you will find it after many days."
Ecclesiastes 11:1

Kidmin matters not only in the present but also for the future because our choices and decisions have a ripple effect that extends beyond our lifetime. In this devotional, we will explore the significance of our investment in children's ministry, understanding that the impact we make today may not be fully realized until years or even generations later. Let us be encouraged to press on, knowing that our labor in the Lord is not in vain.

In our fast-paced world, we often seek immediate results and gratification. However, when it comes to Kidmin, we must remember that the impact we make is not always instantly visible. We may not see the fruits of our labor right away, but our choice to invest in children's lives has a ripple effect that can span across time.

The verse in Ecclesiastes 11:1 encourages us to cast our bread upon the waters, suggesting that we should be generous and invest in the lives of others, even without immediate returns. In the context of kidmin, this reminds us that what we do today can have far-reaching effects in the future. The seeds we plant through teaching, mentoring, and modeling Christ-like behavior may take time to grow and bear fruit.

Just as a stone creates ripples in a pond that expand outward, our influence in Kidmin can create a ripple effect that impacts future generations. The child who learns about God's love and truth in our ministry today may become a parent who raises their own children in the faith. Those children, in turn, may impact their communities and even future generations with the same love and truth they received.

When we choose to invest in children's ministry, we are making a conscious decision to be a part of something bigger than ourselves. We become agents of change, shaping the future by pouring into the lives of children. Our actions, words, and the love we show today can have a lasting impact that shapes the course of individuals, families, and communities for generations to come.

Therefore, let us not be discouraged by the lack of immediate results. Instead, let us be faithful and consistent in our service, knowing that our efforts will leave a lasting legacy. Whether it's teaching a Bible lesson, praying with a child, or simply showing them God's love, every act of kindness and faithfulness has the potential to create a ripple effect that can change the world.:

Dear Heavenly Father, thank You for the privilege of serving in kidmin and investing in the lives of children. Help us to remember that our choices and actions today have a ripple effect that can shape the future. Give us patience, endurance, and faith as we sow seeds of love, truth, and discipleship. May our labor in the Lord not be in vain, but may it produce a bountiful harvest that spans generations. In Jesus' name, we pray. Amen.

Takeaway

Kidmin matters to the future because our choices and decisions have a ripple effect that extends beyond our lifetime. Let us be encouraged to invest in the lives of children, even if we do not see immediate results. The seeds we plant today may take time to grow and bear fruit, impacting future generations with the love and truth of Christ. May we embrace the opportunity to shape the future through our faithful service in Kidmin, knowing that our labor in the Lord is never in vain. IT MATTERS.

_____

_____

_____

_____

_____

_____

_____

_____

_____

KIDS ARE NOT JUST
OBSERVERS; THEY ARE

participants

IN GOD'S AMAZING PLAN.

WEEK 48 : IT MATTERS TO THE FUTURE
In Pursuit of the Well Done: Fulfilling Your Kidmin Calling

"His master replied, 'Well done, good and faithful servant! You have been faithful with a few things; I will put you in charge of many things. Come and share your master's happiness!'"
Matthew 25:21

If you are reading this devotional, chances are you have answered the call to serve in children's ministry. Whether you are a children's pastor, a volunteer, or someone passionate about reaching and teaching children, know that your role is significant and impactful.

Serving in children's ministry is not a coincidence or a mere task. It is a calling from God, a divine assignment that has been entrusted to us. Whether you are a full-time children's pastor or a dedicated volunteer, your role in Kidmin is vital to the Kingdom of God. The children we minister to are not just the future of the Church; they are the Church of today. Their spiritual growth and development are of utmost importance, and we have the privilege of guiding them on their faith journey.

In Matthew 25:21, we find the words of the master commending his servant for being faithful to what was entrusted to him. The same applies to us in our role as children's pastors and volunteers. Our faithfulness in serving the children and families entrusted to our care is recognized by our Heavenly Father. He sees the love, dedication, and effort we pour into shaping young lives, and He promises to reward us for our faithfulness.

Staying faithful to our calling in Kidmin is not always easy. It requires commitment, sacrifice, and perseverance. There may be challenges, setbacks, and moments of weariness along the way. However, we are reminded that our labor in the Lord is not in vain. Every lesson taught, every prayer prayed, and every act of love and kindness shown to a child has eternal significance.

We are called to be faithful in the small things, knowing that God will entrust us with greater things. As children's pastors and volunteers, we have the opportunity to impact the lives of children, shaping their understanding of God, His Word, and His love for them. What we do now has the potential to shape their future and set them on a path of lifelong discipleship.

Moreover, our faithfulness in Kidmin extends beyond our earthly journey. The impact we make in the lives of children has eternal implications. We are not just investing in their present; we are sowing seeds that will bear fruit in eternity. The joy of hearing the words, "Well done, good and faithful servant," echoes in our hearts as we envision the eternal rewards and the lives transformed through our obedience and dedication.

Heavenly Father, thank You for calling us to serve in children's ministry. We pray for strength, wisdom, and perseverance to fulfill our assignment faithfully. Help us to stay focused on the eternal significance of our work, knowing that our labor in the Lord is not in vain. May we be empowered by Your Spirit to impact the lives of children and families, leading them closer to You. In Jesus' name, we pray. Amen.

Takeaway

As children's pastors and volunteers, following the call to serve in Kidmin is an important assignment. Our faithfulness now in teaching, guiding, and loving the children entrusted to us has lasting implications. Let us stay faithful to our calling, knowing that our Heavenly Father sees and rewards our efforts. May we be encouraged by the promise of sharing in our Master's happiness, both in this life and for all eternity. IT MATTERS.

IN CHILDREN'S MINISTRY,
WE ARE
SOWING SEEDS OF

hope

IN THE HEARTS OF
LITTLE ONES.

WEEK 49 : IT MATTERS TO THE FUTURE

Investing in Eternity: Why Kidmin Holds the Key to the Future

"I have fought the good fight, I have finished the race, I have kept the faith."
2 Timothy 4:7

As children's ministry leaders, we have the incredible privilege of shaping the future of kids. Beyond the fun and games, our role holds a profound purpose that carries significant weight. Let us be inspired and encouraged to faithfully fulfill our calling, knowing that the impact we make today will shape the course of many lives in the years to come.

Kidmin is more than just entertaining children; it is a crucial investment in the future. The children we minister to are not just the future of the church; they are the church of today. They carry within them the potential to become passionate followers of Christ, leaders in their communities, and agents of change in the world. Our role as children's ministry leaders is to nurture their faith, equip them with biblical truths, and help them develop a strong foundation for a lifelong relationship with Jesus.

In 2 Timothy 4:7, the apostle Paul reflects on his own journey of faith, proclaiming that he fought the good fight, finished the race, and kept the faith. Likewise, our mission in Kidmin is to guide children on their own journey of faith, preparing them to stand firm in a world that often challenges their beliefs and values. We are called to equip them with God's Word, teach them to navigate difficult situations, and empower them to make godly choices.

The impact we have on children's lives extends far beyond their childhood years. As we invest in their spiritual growth, we are shaping their character, values, and worldview. We are helping to mold future leaders, parents, and influencers who will carry the torch of faith and continue the work of the Kingdom. The seeds we plant today will bear fruit in their lives for years to come.

Furthermore, Kidmin matters to the future of the church. The children we minister to are the future leaders, worshipers, and servants of the body of Christ. By instilling in them a love for God's Word, a passion for worship, and a heart for service, we are building a strong foundation for the church's continued growth and impact. We are raising up a generation that will carry the torch of faith and advance the Kingdom of God.

Kidmin also matters to families, as it provides a supportive environment for parents to nurture their children's spiritual development. As children's ministry leaders, we come alongside families, partnering with parents in the important task of raising godly children. We provide resources, encouragement, and opportunities for families to grow together in their faith. By empowering parents and equipping them to be the primary spiritual influencers in their children's lives, we are strengthening the foundation of the family unit.

Heavenly Father, we thank You for the privilege of serving in children's ministry. Help us to recognize the significance of our role in shaping the future of kids, the church, and families. Strengthen us to faithfully carry out this vital mission, knowing that the impact we make today will have far-reaching effects. May Your Holy Spirit guide and empower us to sow seeds of faith and nurture the hearts of children. In Jesus' name, we pray. Amen.

Takeaway

As children's ministry leaders, we play a critical role in shaping the future of kids. Our impact extends beyond their childhood years, influencing their character, faith, and leadership abilities. Let us be faithful in nurturing their relationship with Jesus, equipping them with biblical truths, and preparing them to make a difference in their world. Remember, the work we do in Kidmin matters not only to the children we serve but also to the future of the church and families. IT MATTERS.

_____

_____

_____

_____

_____

_____

_____

_____

CHILDREN'S MINISTRY
IS WHERE YOUNG MINDS
ENCOUNTER THE
timeless truths
OF GOD'S WORD.

WEEK 50 : IT MATTERS TO THE FUTURE
Seizing the Moment: Kidmin Matters for the Future

"As long as it is day, we must do the works of him who sent me.
Night is coming when no one can work."
John 9:4

In this fast-paced world, time seems to slip through our fingers like sand. We often find ourselves caught up in the busyness of life, unaware of the precious moments passing by. But in the realm of children's ministry, every minute counts. It's a calling that demands our utmost attention, dedication, and passion. Why? Because we have been entrusted with the incredible responsibility of shaping the future of our kids.

The passage in John 9:4 holds a powerful message that resonates deeply with the urgency of our task. These words, spoken by Jesus, remind us of the limited time we have been given to fulfill God's purpose and make an impact in the lives of children.

Each day, as we step into the children's ministry arena, we have an incredible opportunity to sow seeds of faith, love, and hope. We have the privilege of sharing the truth of God's Word, teaching them about Jesus, and guiding them in their spiritual journey. But we must not take this responsibility lightly. The future of these precious young souls hangs in the balance, and we have the power to influence their eternal destiny.

Time is a non-renewable resource. Every minute wasted is a missed opportunity, a moment that can never be reclaimed. Our role as Kidmin leaders is not only to entertain or babysit but to invest in the lives of our kids with intentionality and purpose. We must seize every moment to share the gospel, nurture their faith, and equip them with the spiritual tools they need to navigate the challenges of life.

As we engage with children, we must remember that our time with them is a gift from God. It is a season of divine appointment, a moment to make an eternal impact. Let us be present, fully attentive, and aware of the significance of each interaction. Let us make the most of every opportunity to pour into their lives, to listen to their hearts, and to guide them closer to Jesus.

Furthermore, the urgency of our task compels us to work diligently and faithfully. The night is coming when our ability to work may be hindered. We do not know what lies ahead, but we know that today is the day to labor for the kingdom. Let us not delay or procrastinate, but let us be committed to using our time, energy, and resources wisely for the sake of the children entrusted to us.

Dear friend, the future depends on the investments we make today. Every minute we spend with our kids in children's ministry matters. It is an opportunity to shape lives, build foundations, and cultivate a love for Jesus that will endure. So let us embrace this divine calling with passion, purpose, and a deep sense of urgency. The time is now, and the impact we make today will resonate far into the future.

Dear Heavenly Father, we come before You with grateful hearts, recognizing the weight of the responsibility You have entrusted to us in children's ministry. We thank You for the privilege of shaping the future of our kids and for allowing us to be instruments of Your love and truth. Lord, help us to be mindful of the limited time we have been given and the urgency of the task at hand. Grant us wisdom, strength, and discernment as we pour into the lives of these young ones. Fill us with Your Holy Spirit, that we may seize every moment, making the most of our time with them. May Your Word take root in their hearts, transforming them into disciples who will impact the world for Your glory. In Jesus' name, we pray. Amen.

Takeaway

As we reflect on the importance of investing our time in children's ministry, let us remember that every minute counts. Each moment we spend with our kids is an opportunity to sow seeds of faith, love, and hope. The future depends on the investments we make today. Therefore, let us embrace this calling with passion and a deep sense of urgency. May we seize every moment, pouring into the lives of our kids, sharing the gospel, and equipping them for the challenges they will face. Let us be faithful stewards of the time God has given us, making the most of every opportunity to shape lives and build a foundation that will last. Remember, time is a gift, and how we use it in children's ministry matters for eternity. IT MATTERS.

_____

_____

_____

_____

_____

_____

_____

_____

KIDS ARE NOT JUST
RECIPIENTS; THEY ARE
CARRIERS OF
God's blessings.

WEEK 51 : IT MATTERS TO THE FUTURE
Kidmin Matters to the Future: A Lifetime of Service to Jesus

"Let the little children come to me and do not hinder them, for the kingdom of God belongs to such as these."
Luke 18:16

It is said that children are the future, and indeed they are. They hold within them the potential to serve Jesus and make a lasting difference in the world. DL Moody once wisely stated, "If I could relive my life, I would devote my entire ministry to reaching children for God!" This quote encapsulates the heart of why Kidmin matters—because children have their whole lives ahead of them to serve Jesus.

Kids have their whole lives ahead of them—a vast expanse of time to grow in their faith, develop their gifts, and fulfill God's purposes. It is a journey that begins in childhood and extends throughout their lifetime. Our role as Kidmin leaders is to nurture and equip them, instilling in them a foundation rooted in the love and truth of Jesus Christ.

In Luke 18:16, Jesus said, "Let the little children come to me and do not hinder them, for the kingdom of God belongs to such as these." These words from our Savior remind us of the immense value He places on children. He recognizes their openness, teachable hearts, and potential for Kingdom impact.

As we invest our time, resources, and energy in children's ministry, we are sowing seeds that will bear fruit for years to come. We have the privilege of sharing the Gospel with these young hearts, imparting biblical truths, and guiding them on their journey of faith. What we do today will shape their understanding of who God is and what it means to follow Him.

DL Moody's quote echoes a deep truth—that reaching children for God is a calling of utmost importance. It is a call to prioritize their spiritual development, recognizing that they have the capacity to change the world through their devotion to Jesus. By investing in their lives now, we are setting them on a trajectory of lifelong service to the Lord.

Psalm 71:17-18 says, "Since my youth, God, you have taught me, and to this day I declare your marvelous deeds. Even when I am old and gray, do not forsake me, my God, till I declare your power to the next generation, your mighty acts to all who are to come." This passage emphasizes the intergenerational nature of faith and the responsibility we have to pass on God's truths to the next generation.

Kidmin Friend, as we reflect on the importance of children's ministry to the future, let us be filled with a sense of purpose and urgency. Let us embrace the privilege of sowing seeds of faith in the lives of our children, knowing that the impact we make today will shape their journey with Jesus for years to come.

May we always remember that children have their whole lives ahead of them, and our investment in their spiritual growth matters. Let us commit ourselves to guiding, teaching, and equipping them with a strong foundation in Christ. And as we do so, may we echo the words of DL Moody, dedicating our lives to reaching children for God.

Heavenly Father, we thank You for the incredible privilege of serving in children's ministry. Help us to recognize the immense potential that lies within each child's life. Fill us with passion and wisdom as we invest our time and energy in nurturing their faith. May we be faithful in equipping them to serve You all the days of their lives. In Jesus' name, we pray. Amen.

Takeaway

As we consider the importance of children's ministry to the future, let us be reminded of the significant role we play in shaping young lives. Each moment we invest in nurturing their faith is an opportunity to ignite a life-long commitment to serving Jesus. May we approach our role with passion, perseverance, and unwavering faith, trusting that God will use our efforts to impact future generations. Let us seize the opportunity to sow seeds of truth and love, knowing that our labor in the Lord is never in vain. May we be inspired by DL Moody's words and commit ourselves wholeheartedly to reaching children for God, knowing that through our dedication, the future will be filled with faithful servants of Jesus Christ. IT MATTERS.

IN CHILDREN'S MINISTRY,
WE HAVE THE INCREDIBLE
PRIVILEGE OF
investing in eternity.

WEEK 52 : IT MATTERS TO THE FUTURE
Eternity Matters: Why Kidmin Holds Eternal Significance

"What is your life?
For you are a mist that appears for a little time and then vanishes."
James 4:14

Have you ever stopped to think about the brevity of life? The truth is, our time on this earth is but a fleeting moment, like a vapor that appears for a little while and then vanishes away. James 4:14 reminds us of this sobering reality.

As children's ministry leaders, we have the privilege and responsibility of shaping the lives of young ones. We invest countless hours, pouring our hearts and souls into teaching them about Jesus, planting seeds of faith, and nurturing their spiritual growth. And while our impact in this present life is significant, it is the eternal consequences that truly matter.

Kidmin matters for the future because it is not just about the here and now; it is about preparing children for eternity. Our role is to point them to Jesus, the way, the truth, and the life. We have the incredible opportunity to share the good news of salvation with them, teaching them that placing their faith in Christ secures their eternal destiny.

As we consider the brevity of life and the weight of eternity, let us approach our calling with a renewed sense of urgency and purpose. May we prioritize the proclamation of the Gospel and the transformational power of God's Word in the lives of children. Let us strive to lead them into a personal relationship with Jesus, teaching them to love and follow Him wholeheartedly.

Heavenly Father, we come before You with hearts burdened by the reality of life's brevity. Help us to remember that our time on this earth is short, and eternity awaits. Give us a sense of urgency as we minister to children, knowing that our impact reaches far beyond the present moment. Fill us with Your love and wisdom as we guide young hearts toward You. Empower us by Your Spirit to faithfully sow seeds of faith and cultivate a longing for eternity in the hearts of these precious children. In Jesus' name, we pray. Amen.

Takeaway

Today, let us be reminded that our work in children's ministry has eternal implications. We have the privilege of impacting the lives of children and pointing them to Jesus, who offers eternal life. Let us invest our time, energy, and resources wisely, knowing that the seeds we sow today will bear fruit in eternity. May we be faithful stewards of this calling, recognizing the weight of eternity and the incredible privilege we have to lead children into a personal relationship with Christ. Let us seize every opportunity to make a lasting difference in their lives, keeping our eyes fixed on the eternal rewards that await us. IT MATTERS.

_____

_____

_____

_____

_____

_____

_____

_____

_____

CONCLUSION:

Dear Kidmin Friend,

As we come to the end of this journey exploring why Kidmin matters, I want to take a moment to encourage you and remind you of the tremendous impact your role as a children's ministry leader or volunteer has in the lives of kids, families, the church, the community, and the world. What you do matters—more than you may ever fully realize.

Throughout these devotionals, we have delved into the various reasons why Kidmin matters, exploring the heart of God, the importance to the church, the impact on families, the significance for kids, the influence on the community and the world, and the eternal weight of our efforts. We have seen how the power of the Gospel, love, discipleship, and community intertwine to shape the lives of children and leave a lasting legacy.

You have been entrusted with a sacred calling—a calling that extends far beyond teaching lessons and organizing activities. You have been given the privilege to partner with God in raising a generation of children who will know Him, love Him, and serve Him. You have the opportunity to sow seeds of faith, hope, and love that will bear fruit not only in this present time but also in eternity.

It is not always an easy task. You may face challenges, doubts, and moments of weariness. But let me remind you that your labor is not in vain. Your faithfulness, dedication, and love for God and His little ones make an eternal difference. Every prayer, every lesson, every smile, and every act of kindness matters more than you can fathom.

So, as you reflect on the importance of Kidmin, remember that you are not alone. You are part of a vast network of Kidmin leaders and volunteers who share the same passion and commitment. Reach out to them, encourage one another, and glean wisdom from their experiences. If you are not currently a part of KidzMatter's I Love Kidmin Facebook community, it's time to get involved! Together, we can support and uplift each other in this incredible journey.

I want to leave you with this encouragement: keep pressing on, keep sowing seeds, and keep loving and leading the children entrusted to your care. Your work matters. It matters to God, it matters to the church, it matters to families, it matters to kids, it matters to your community and the world, and it matters for the future.

May you continue to walk in the grace, strength, and wisdom that God abundantly provides. May you see the beauty of His work unfolding in the lives of the children you serve. And may you be filled with joy and satisfaction as you witness the impact of your ministry both in this life and for all eternity.

Thank you for your heart, dedication, and unwavering commitment to Kidmin. May you be blessed as you continue to be a vessel of God's love and grace.

It truly matters so much!

XO,
Beth

Printed in the USA
CPSIA information can be obtained
at www.ICGtesting.com
JSHW011116240923
48734JS00004B/8